COMFORTABLE CHRISTIANITY

Volume 1: Examining hypocrisy through the eyes of a hypocrite

by
Caleb Seifu

Illustrated by
Dag Haile

Edited by
Lindsay Morris

ISBN-13: 978-0692465707

Cover Design by Dag Haile

ComfortableChristianity.com

In loving memory of Jon Randles

TABLE OF CONTENTS

YOU'RE GOING TO HELL, BRO:
A satirical introduction

When I think of all the people destined to eternal hellfire, as a Christian, I am faced with two polar opposite options: 1) convert/save them, or 2) be heartless, and mind my own business – simply accept the fact that everyone is going to hell.

My neighbor? *Hell.* My co-worker? *Hell.* My bartender? *Hell.*

The irreligious may argue, "Everyone's going to hell; therefore, it should be a cool place." They fancy themselves learning guitar with Jimmy Hendrix, flirting with Marilyn Monroe, and attending (non-hologram) Tupac concerts. But the joke is on them – *Tupac was Catholic!* They'll be at his hologram concerts after all. (Note: This assumption varies, as some Protestants believe Catholics are going to hell.)

Regardless of the Tupac snub, to non-believers, hell may still seem like Utopia–*they're finally free of Christians!* A moment of cooling relief comes to a sudden halt when the most irritating Comfortable Christian – one who used faith as he/she found fit – becomes their bunkmate. *Now this* is hell.

God – although omnipresent – chooses not to be there. This means the hell-bound may potentially be able to continue their (now literally) *heated debate* about God's existence; perhaps even *fire up* new theories on evolutionary adaptation – given their radically different environment.

Why is this Christian here? Well, to God, sin comes from the heart, not the action. So being seemingly virtuous is merely a deceptive masquerade.

As much as I hate to admit it, the truth is, only God can judge. (Although I have a list of suggestions if He calls me to His administrative cabinet.) My faith in Jesus doesn't require me to judge everyone; sadly, it forbids it! It requires me to allow Him to transform my life, making me the type of person a non-believer would admire. Jesus said, "In the same way, let your light shine before others, that they may see your good deeds and glorify your Father in heaven." (Matthew 5:16)

But many of us have stalled this transformation. We've dimmed the light from shining – ultimately, curtailing the glorification of the Father. All the while, we claim to be His sons and daughters.

This journey, an introspective look at hypocrisy, began when I looked in the mirror and said to my reflection, "According to my religious beliefs, you're going to hell, bro."

PRELUDE

Although this read is directed to Christians, the concept is universal –almost everyone has been affected by Christianity. At age 29, I examined my life. Like many Christians, I had practiced faith selectively, somehow comfortable with contradiction. I failed to see how egregiously (and sometimes comically) I was misrepresenting Christ.

I began writing in a self-reflective manner, examining the finer points of hypocrisy. I am driven by the notion that I have *fooled myself* into thinking that I'm saved. And I doubt that I'm alone.

Everyone knows (or thinks they know) who Jesus is. Whether they go to church, used to go to church, or would never go to church, everyone has a pretty good idea who Jesus is based on the disingenuous ways Christianity has been practiced. Have we encountered Jesus, *or something else?* Are we His followers, *or something else?*

The mission of this book is three-fold. The first objective is to examine hypocrisy through the eyes of a hypocrite. The second objective is to explore genuine faith. The final objective is to encourage and compel transformation, beginning with my own.

We all struggle with insecurity – from the teenage girl desperately trying to show cleavage, to the macho man desperately trying to hide it. Even those who seem to be perfect, or portray themselves as such, have their insecurities. As we age, we reassure ourselves that we've either 'still got it' or that it doesn't matter. *But of course, it matters.*

Each morning we examine ourselves in the mirror, correcting and re-correcting until we're satisfied, or come to the realization that we won't be. Even our 'selfies' serve as on-the-go mirrors. After examining numerous shots, we filter and post one. It's what we want to represent us, even if it doesn't always reflect us.

"Examine yourselves to see if your faith is genuine." 2 Corinthians 13:5

We can't assume that we look fine based on last week's reflection, so how can we consider our faith to be genuine without regular examination? The absence of prayer, reflection through the Word, and the existence of willful sin should result in a struggle with insecurity. Instead, we reassure ourselves that it's okay, or it doesn't matter. *But of course it matters.*

Imagine life without our own reflections. Grooming or applying makeup would make us look even more ridiculous. And that's exactly what religion does.

The world scoffs at our hypocrisy. *Who are we trying to fool?* We want Christ's image to represent us, even if it doesn't always reflect us.

PART 1:
FIRST IMPRESSIONS

THE HANGOVER

"Do not get drunk on wine, which leads to debauchery. Instead, be filled with the Spirit." Ephesians 5:18

I woke up groggy, my head pounding and sensitive to the smallest darkness. Yes, darkness. What just happened? Another spiritual hangover from the youth camp I attended. *It was a blast for sure.* It's inspiring to be surrounded by like-minded individuals, with nothing to focus on but praising God (and that cutie praising God).

There's music, drama, and the Word. We wake up to Jesus, go to sleep to Jesus, *wow!* I finally understood the cliché, "Christianity isn't a religion; it's a relationship." And by relationship, I mean *a fling!* Complete with a rush of overwhelming, yet short-lived emotional euphoria.

Many Christians can recall a moment or multiple moments when they decided to truly follow Jesus. And for those raised in church, this experience often happens at camp. Think of it as 'Coachella' or 'Burning Man' for Jesus freaks.

As a professional camp-goer, a seasoned attendee of these youth-worship-revival conferences, I had built my tolerance. I went because my friends were Christian, and they went. It was more of a social thing, especially when you take into consideration that, although some of us were praising the Most High, some of us were getting the most high!

I had experienced the unsmooth transition, the shaky handling, and ultimate crash and burn caused by switching gears back into the *real world* from my Jesus-buzz. It led me to the conclusion to never allow myself to get that drunk in the Spirit again. All the while, I tried to maintain remnants of Christian consciousness.

'Ain't no party like a Holy Ghost party, cause a Holy Ghost party'… just stopped. For days we'd been engulfed in the presence of God, binging on the Spirit. But now it's time to get back to real life. We've got things to do. We dap up Jesus, "Alright then, God, it's been real. No, tomorrow's not good for me, how 'bout next conference?"

They call it a retreat, a time to scale back and to focus on Jesus. But He doesn't want our retreat; He wants our surrender – the unconditional submission and death of our will. We retreat when we're momentarily overwhelmed, but may soon resurge. Instead of making permanent changes, we opt for temporary fixes. This is akin to treating a diseased heart to a few days off in the form of veggie juicing. But next week, *a buffet cruise!*

THE OPIATE OF THE MASSES

At these retreats, not only is there enough 'God' to pass around (our cup overfloweth), there's even peer pressure to dive in. We're actually the odd ones out if our hands *aren't* lifted in worship. And it's easy to get high off of God when He's cheap, easily accessible, and all of our friends are doing Him.

As we transition back to work or school, we're spiritually sensitive to everything around us. The music we used to listen to, things we used to watch, things we used to do – all pierce our spirits deeply. We try to avoid them. But eventually the hangover begins to fade as our eyes, ears, and hearts get accustomed to the darkness.

It's the simple economics of supply and demand. Let's say there are ten thirsty patrons and twenty drinks; the cost of refreshment is cheap. But if the number of available drinks was reduced to only five, the price goes up. The patrons will have to decide if they're *really* thirsty.

At a conference, the demand of those seeking Jesus is high, but the supply is even higher. There may be multiple services and activities daily. When it's over, our demand may still be high, but there are no morning, mid-day, or evening services. The price of seeking God just skyrocketed. Now we have to decide if we're *really* thirsty.

WOLF PACK DEMOGRAPHICS

"I am sending you out like sheep among wolves. Therefore be as shrewd as snakes and as innocent as doves." Matthew 10:16

The conference experience may have only served to build our tolerance to God. Once we get back to the real world, we realize that we never really changed. When the high runs out, we may find ourselves to be *in the church but not of it.*

I was driving home to a predominately black neighborhood in Los Angeles when I spotted a rare sight: two Caucasians. I was torn between whether I should take a picture or assist them with escaping. Perhaps they were Jehovah's Witnesses, undercover cops, or victims of a faulty GPS. Whatever the case, it was clear to me that they were 'in the hood but not of the hood'.

This became a reoccurring anomaly, a result of gentrification. I welcomed the thought of renewing rundown neighborhoods, businesses, and public properties – stopping short of my own pending displacement.

When the character of 'the hood' changes, can we still call it 'the hood'?

The Early Church was a community in which you had to be willing to die for your faith. But as Christianity became mainstream, moving in became desirable. *But so much has changed.* It's no longer an anomaly to see un-Christ-like people in the church. There may have been a time when I would be perceived as 'not of this church,' but so many in this church are like me.

When the character of the church changes, can we still call it the church?

In the *Parable of the Tares*, an enemy plants weeds among the wheat. But the master doesn't pluck them out because their roots may be woven together. This means the weeds grow with the wheat, and perhaps fool themselves into thinking that they too, are the wheat.

It's not until the harvest that they are separated. So it should come as no surprise that there are, and will always be, false-hearted, fraudulent, and hypocritical people in the church.

The surprise was that I was one of them.

Please allow me to formally introduce myself; I'm your Comfort Counselor. My role is to help you justify yourself in defense of sound biblical doctrine with the use of loose interpretations, logical fallacies, and selective hearing. As a 'devil's advocate' (pardon the pun), I specialize in loopholes and out-of-context scripture. Since I will be representing both sides, conservative and liberal, I may occasionally contradict myself. *It's what I do, baby!*

NEVER AGAIN

The glaring problem with discipleship is that it requires discipline. But we want God to reinforce our good behavior with a steady flow of rewards, much like a dog. *Roll,* treat. *Shake,* treat. *Do not bear false witness,* treat. "God, if you give me this (fill-in-the-blank), I'll quit this (fill-in-the-blank)." And if it seems like He isn't responding, then what's the point of obedience? Jesus is Lord! – *if He's giving treats!*

'Jesus take the wheel' is much easier in karaoke than in practice. Unless, of course, the 'wheel' we're referring to is a flat tire. *It usually is.* It's preferable that He rides shotgun, a co-pilot on stand-by, just in case we need Him.

Just like a binge drinker turns to substance in time of hardship, we turn to God in ours; or we do both. (Jesus Cuervo, *anyone?*) Eventually we'll clean up our act, and sober up. Just as we're encouraged to 'go easy' on the liquor, we 'go easy' on God.

If you've ever had a hangover, the last thing you want to do is drink more. *Usually.* I can't speak for everyone, but next time, you'll be watching your intake, thinking to yourself, "never again." Likewise, I never again allowed myself to get spiritually hammered only to wake up to real life. Getting 'drunk in the Spirit' wasn't practical. So as a teenager, I decided to follow Jesus from afar. I watched my friends go cuckoo for Christ – some of whom are no longer in the faith. For the next 10 years I took a pass. I was a spiritual designated driver – cruising through Christianity.

THE PASSION OF THE CHRISTIAN

Every once in a while, a faith-based movie hits the box office, and we rally in support. *We are Christians, hear us roar!* And seek whom we may devour —which for now is M&M's, popcorn, and soda.

We usually go to the movies to watch sex and violence... so it's refreshing to cleanse our palate with the latest Jesus movie. None are more notable than Mel Gibson's *The Passion of the Christ*. At 25th all-time box office sales, its viewing was like a rite of passage for Christians.

People cried, even got saved in the theatres. The movie was so touching that it overshadowed Gibson's racist, anti-Semitic, and profane remarks. He may have been able to depict the Passion of the Christ on the silver screen, but not on the evening news.

But who am I to judge? I too, behaved hypocritically. And although I considered myself a Christian, I wanted nothing to do with the movie. *Why?* It would evoke too much emotion – something I had previously encountered at Jesus camp. My Christian friends would watch it, cry, get on a spiritual high, and then come back down to my level. I found it more practical to stay down.

I wasn't willing to live for Jesus, so the last thing I wanted was to be haunted by images of Him dying for me. If viewing God's love leads one to offer his/her life in return (Romans 12:1), I'd rather avoid the idea. *And I'm not alone.* Many of us like or even associate ourselves with Christ, yet suppress the thought of His sacrifice – His passion for humanity. The attitude concedes that Jesus may have died for me, but I won't live for Him.

Gandhi liked Christ, but not Christians, because Christians often fail to share the same spirit, the same attributes, the same passion. This sentiment is shared by many non-believers, and it leads them to question the faith altogether.

It should lead us to question our faith, or rather, how we practice it. We often lack the passion to walk in His spirit or the guts to flatly deny Him. We ease our minds by saying, "I'm not perfect," and neither do we strive to be (Matthew 5:48).

40 OUNCES TO FREEDOM

There are so many ways people spend $20 to ease their minds. One may buy a 12-pack of beer, a sack of herb, or get a cheap quickie massage. (Caution: other $20 cheap quickies may result in a venereal disease.) I have found short-term peace in all of the above (aside from the one that may cause venereal disease), but none gave me more peace than throwing $20 into the church's offering bucket.

Passing the offering can be a brief yet uncomfortable moment if you're not giving. It's like a hot potato. I could either carefully time my arrival at church to miss it, or I could just toss in $20.

As a child, I was taught that 10% of my income goes to the Lord. I could bear this with a meager allowance, *but now I have bills!* (which may include a 12-pack of beer, a sack of herb, and a quickie massage).

Although $20 wasn't 10% of my income, putting it in the offering did two things:

1. **It showed others that I was giving.** *Appearance is very important to a superficial Christian.*
2. **It made me feel better about myself.** *This minuscule concession somehow eased my mind.*

It made perfect sense that I could give God my life, but not my 10%. When the ushers came, I'd toss in my crumbs. I completely missed the point; tithing isn't about money.

Giving mirrors how invested we are to Christ's cause. (Granted, 'Christ's cause' isn't to furnish the pastor with a diamond-studded Rolex.) It reflects the way we take Monday through Saturday for ourselves — ignore God and how He wants us to live — then give Him Sunday. *Excuse me, Sunday morning.* We toss in a couple crumbs of our time, of our will, of our lives to God and it eases our minds.

THE MASQUERADE BALL

We can think of so many excuses not to give. But the main one is that the church has enough money. Some *unfairly* implicate the pastor, *simply because* his car payment dwarfs their mortgage. Some say that religion is big business; *there's no doubt that it is.*

"For such people are false apostles, deceitful workers, masquerading as apostles of Christ. And no wonder, for Satan himself masquerades as an angel of light. It is not surprising, then, if his servants also masquerade as servants of righteousness." 2 Corinthians 11:13-15

Wherever there's money involved, there will be those who seek to profit. Consider the profiteers in the temple who Jesus drove out with a whip. Consider the false preachers that were banking while Paul, the greatest apostle, worked as a tent maker. Consider how Judas, one of Jesus' carefully chosen disciples, betrayed Him for profit.

Just as there are false prophets, there are false congregations. Their leaders tell them whatever their itching ears want to hear (2 Timothy 4:3). Jesus warned us that frauds would come in His name, seeking to make their own followers. So we can't dis-

15

count Christ on the grounds that we have encountered a stunt double. He specifically warned us that there would be many.

"In their greed these teachers will exploit you with fabricated stories."
2 Peter 2:3

We've seen it all: from fake healings to fake prophecies. Many leaders are not praying for people; they're preying on people. On one occasion, a 'prophet' who insisted that he lay hands on me, whispered in my ear, "just fall." I resisted. I wasn't about to fake being 'slain in the Spirit,' regardless of how aggressively he pressed against my forehead. Fortunately, my gym routine hadn't neglected the neck muscles. *Then he did the unthinkable.* As he closed in, anointing me with a double portion of projectile saliva, he strategically placed his foot behind my heel. *Push.* I stumbled backwards, narrowly escaping being 'slain in the flesh.'

We can identify false teachers and followers by what they value. If one values something more than merely following Jesus, then Christ is merely a platform for profit, ambition, or physical satisfaction. For example, something is wrong if your leader tells you to 'plant a seed,' even if it's your rent money, to just trust God! Don't think He failed you because you weren't repaid "pressed down, shaken together, and running over."

In that sort of scenario, you were in it for the money, just like your leader. Perhaps you should've inquired about what services the church's homeless ministry would provide you with, in the event that God doesn't keep His promise.

If we have material motives, we become like Judas. Just as he sealed the betrayal with a kiss, we seal our betrayal with the public appearance that we love Jesus. (We really love money). Giving is something done out of a cheerful heart, not begrudgingly, not to avoid feeling guilty and, under no circumstance, to get a return on our investment.

LUKE(WARM), I AM NOT YOUR FATHER

When it comes to beverage options, everyone has their own preference. However, one thing we can all agree on is that we want our drinks either hot or cold. No coffee shop can stay afloat if it's serving lukewarm lattes.

So, what do you do if you're looking for that perfect something to trigger a gag reflex? Well, you let it sit and conform to the room temperature.

"So, because you are lukewarm – neither hot nor cold – I am about to spit you out of my mouth." Revelation 3:16

When we first accept Jesus, we do it because we're overwhelmed by the urgency. As we make our way to the altar to recite the Sinner's Prayer, we never think that this feeling will just fade away. And then over time, we let our faith sit and conform to the world.

We try to keep the spark alive, while limiting it to a spark. Obviously, we don't want to be cold to Jesus. So we end up in that middle ground, that perfect spot that triggers His gag reflex.

Many of us are lukewarm, Comfortable Christians. And we've surrounded ourselves with other lukewarm Christians. Instead of challenging each other to be more like our Savior, we have a false sense of safety-in-numbers. Did we ever have a desire to reflect Jesus? *Of course we did.* We just let that sit.

There may have been a time when our zeal for Jesus was great, when we had a passion for Him. At some point we wanted to reflect Him. Instead, we begin reflecting the people around us.

"Then Jesus answered, 'Will you really lay down your life for me? Very truly I tell you, before the rooster crows, you will disown me three times!'" John 13:38

Peter loved Jesus so much he was willing to die for Him – fight and die, that is. When the soldiers came to arrest Jesus, Peter attacked one, severing his ear. Then Jesus did the unthinkable: he rebuked Peter and healed the soldier... and laid down His life.

Imagine for a moment that you are Peter. Jesus had just predicted that you would disown Him, and here you are proving that you won't. Bravely, you, a fisherman, attack a professional soldier for Jesus – only to be verbally reprimanded.

You were reprimanded because you failed to represent Jesus. You see, we attack who we perceive to be the enemy, while Jesus seeks to heal who we perceive to be the enemy. Does our faith heal or hurt our enemies?

Just like Peter, we often find ourselves unable to lay our lives down. We may: a) disown Him under social pressure, b) disown Him by attacking social adversity, or c) disown Him by seeking material and social status.

There are so many ways to disown Jesus. But ultimately, we do it by misrepresenting His passion, just as Peter did. Will we really lay down our lives for Him, or are we contributing to the problem?

THE ENCOUNTER

I drove by a big billboard that read, "There is no God." Wow! I'm no stranger to the ills of religion, but I didn't realize that atheists wanted to bite back with a gospel of their own. *"No hope!"* Some atheists have militant congregations, possibly comprised of ex-Christians who have lifted the veil of faith, in exchange for one of human reason.

For Christians, it's pretty agitating to witness the passion of atheist activism. They seemingly troll around suing local governments, forcing them to remove anything with a faith-based connotation—even cross memorials! Their dream is to fulfill the *Separation of Church and State* to the point where it severs the country from its 'Christian-Judeo' background. (Which wouldn't be so bad, as later discussed in *The Last Stone*.)

Clearly, they're our enemies! Their blood boils against us, and our blood boils back! But no atheist hates Christians as passionately as Saul of Tarsus did. No atheist will be as zealously against the inconceivable fairytale in which a crucified man rises from the dead *for your sins* as Saul!

Saul vehemently hated Christians and went on tour searching to imprison and kill them. The Gestapo before the Gestapo, he did everything in his power to find and eradicate them. He was the first anti-Christian activist.

THE ENEMIES OF GOD

Contrary to belief, atheists are not the enemy. We often see their activism as a direct threat. After all, they blaspheme and mock the God of the Bible! But the God of the Bible says, "The name of God is blasphemed among the Gentiles because of you" (Romans 2:24). Wait... what? *Christians are the enemy?!*

The enemies of God aren't people who are passionately against Him; they're people who use Him for what they're passionately against! They use Jesus to endorse themselves. The real enemy of the church is within the church – a religious spirit that allows us to be adherents of something we aren't truly passionate about – the love of Jesus.

"You give a tenth of your spices – mint, dill and cumin. But you have neglected the more important matters of the law – justice, mercy and faithfulness." Matthew 23:23

I'm willing to bet (my tithes and offering) that most atheists wouldn't mind Christians as much if we were more like Christ. *They may still think we're idiots,* but we're loving, kind, and peaceful idiots. In fact, they may appreciate us – even support causes that we would have 'crusaded' for – anti-discrimination, social welfare, and justice.

It was the religious leaders who hated Jesus, not the pagan Romans. Governor Pontius Pilate even appealed on Christ's behalf. "'Why? What crime has he committed?'" asked Pilate. But they shouted all the louder, "'Crucify him!'"(Matthew 27:23). Can you picture Christians being appealed for on the behalf heathens, atheists, and whoever else we've had in our crosshairs? What if atheists could say, "What crime have Christians committed?" Well, it's too late for that.

 **Tip** Have you ever been criticized for being against gays, against social welfare, against birth control, against etcetera? Stand firm! *Especially against 'etcetera'!*

Somehow, the same religious type that cried, "Crucify him," have become His representation. *How 'bout that!* Sure,

Jesus said that we would be hated by the world, but not for being self-righteous!

Has religion caused cultural strife? We've made non-believers intolerant of our intolerance, which is also intolerance. But they can't see that because they so passionately hate us.

Have Christians made the world worse? Have we brought darkness, not light – driving people away from Jesus? Who knew, the whole time the enemy of God, the instrument of hate, was Comfortable Christianity – the use of Christ to support our causes. It's us, Christians, who are persecuting Jesus.

GOOD COP, BAD COP

Let's face it. In the past several centuries, Christianity was spread through the world in 'Good-Cop, Bad-Cop' fashion. Just the way the 'good cop' coerces compliance by 'compassionately' stopping the beating doled out by the 'bad cop', missionaries compassionately imposed their religion upon the remnants of crusading, colonizing, and conquistador-ing invasions.

The 'Good-Cop, Bad-Cop' tactic is really effective in making a suspect talk, and making a pagan a Christian. But before you and a friend go witnessing – one assaulting a nonbeliever, the other coming to his aid with the Gospel –consider this: what kind of believers have been produced by this tactic? It makes adherents that are held to the faith *by fear*. The fear of going to jail is much like the fear of going to hell, in the sense that, once one overcomes the fear, the cop, or the proselytizer, is powerless.

Like many kids, I dealt with bullies growing up. I complied with their abuse until I realized that all they had was fear. *The worst they could do is hit me.*

Is 'fear' all the church has to keep us in line? Is religion just a big bully controlling the masses? Kids raised in church comply until they're no longer afraid of hell. *"Is that all you got God, hell?"* Perhaps it would be more effective to tell them that God's wrath will jam their Internet.

God has not given us the spirit of fear, but of power, love, and a sound mind (2 Timothy 1:7). Perhaps the encounter we've had is not with Jesus, but with religious fear. Christ is merely a means to escape hell. When we're no longer scared, Christ is no longer relevant — our encounter with Him was not based on love for Him.

GOING BLIND

"He fell to the ground and heard a voice say to him, 'Saul, Saul, why do you persecute me?' 'Who are you, Lord?' Saul asked. 'I am Jesus, whom you are persecuting,' he replied." Acts 9:4-5

Saul was on a bloodthirsty, anti-Christ mission. Suddenly, the subject of his persecution rendered him blind for three days. Like him, our encounter with Jesus has blinded us. Wait... what? What about our favorite idiom: "I was blind but now I see"?

I often wonder if that saying is used as frequently in the circles of blind Christians. Either way, the idea is, "I was spiritually unaware of my sin, but now I walk in the light." *Right?* After all, we view non-believers as if they're the blind. They may unknowingly walk in darkness, but we do it on purpose!

People who are blind to Jesus can still be good, respect others, and have morals. They may even live better than Christians. This is especially true when those believers have not encountered Christ, but instead, have encountered religious fear, tradition, emotion, and social belonging.

THE POWER OUTAGE

"Jesus said, 'For judgment I have come into this world, so that the blind will see and those who see will become blind.'" John 9:39

What's to be said about those who have seen the light, but haven't become the light? Consider this: a blind man may be able to use the help of the seeing to navigate through a building. But what if there's a power outage? When all the hallways and rooms go dark, the one with vision can no longer lead. *But he may still try to lead.* The blind man is better off without him. He's been walking in darkness his whole life.

"Some Pharisees who were with him heard him say this and asked, 'What? Are we blind too?'" John 9:40

Like them, we're often clinging to dead religion. We think we still have the moral high-ground, failing to see that our faith is not only blind, but it's powerless without the love of Christ. People we call sinners are better off than us. In fact, they're better off without us!

If one has encountered a false Jesus, they can only profess false faith. Jesus said, "You will know my followers by their fruit." Many who think they're following Jesus are only blinding the world with misrepresentations, dimming His sacred heart – His love for all humanity.

"The eye is the lamp of the body. If your eyes are healthy, your whole body will be full of light. But if your eyes are unhealthy, your whole body will be full of darkness. If then the light within you is darkness, how great is that darkness!" Matthew 6:22-23

The Pharisees thought they were the closest to God, but they were the furthest. The light they thought they had was darkness. And the god they served was fear, tradition, and social status. They never allowed their faith to transform them; instead, they transformed their faith. *We do the same today.*

DIM AND DIMMER

By no stretch of the imagination am I a 'handy guy'. So when one of my four kitchen lights flickered out, I didn't even attempt to replace it. It was no big deal.

After a couple months, a second light flickered out. *Crap.* The visibility in the kitchen was now significantly reduced. This time I couldn't just ignore it.

I just ignored it.

After a couple more months, a third light flickered out. I had to do something! I replaced a bulb and proudly stood back—it fell out and shattered on the floor. This is what I get for trying!

The last light remained for a very long time. For months I operated in dimness, and it correlated with the ease of kitchen cleaning. Who needs four lights? Pfft.

Then one day, I stepped into the kitchen and flipped the switch. Nothing. Oh crap! The fourth and final light was out. I stood there for a moment, in the darkness — realizing that, over the course of a year, I had allowed all of the lights to flicker out!

Meh, whatever.

I was in a huge rush to make a gourmet sandwich, coffee, and have snack-time. The dining area's lights were on, and the reflection was just enough for me to navigate through the kitchen without the use of infrared goggles. Nice!

I marveled while eating the gourmet sandwich, sipping coffee, and enjoying snack-time. How did I allow myself to get to this point? My lights were completely out, yet it didn't bother me enough.

Enough! I decided to replace not one, but all of my kitchen lights!

I put in two.

I wanted to see what it was going to be like. Flip on.

My eyes, my eyes! I felt like a deer in headlights, in a kitchen. I flipped it off. This was terrible! How can I cook and clean in this, *this light*?!

I considered taking one out — going back to one of the four. But there was a point in my life when I operated with all four lights. What changed?

I decided to keep the two lights in and let my eyes adjust. The first thing I noticed was that my kitchen was filthy. There were crumbs on the floor, crumbs on the counter, crumbs on crumbs! Utensils were out of place, and there was even some damage to the wood cabinet. WTF! [fudge]

I spent the next hour cleaning, amazed at how 'okay' everything seemed when I didn't look at it with, you know, light.

"If you were blind, you would not be guilty of sin; but now that you claim you can see, your guilt remains." John 9:41

Christians often claim to have the light — Jesus Christ — but we have conveniently allowed His presence in our lives to diminish. At first it seems minimal; it's no big deal. But as Christ continues to become less and less relevant in our lives, we become less and less aware of the problem.

Many of us have allowed Jesus to completely flicker out. We ultimately operate under the reflections from someone else's light, if at all. All the while, things seem fine. The question is, do we do something about it, or are we comfortable without it?

PSYCHOTIC FAITH

After Saul encountered Jesus, he became like Jesus. He loved all, Jews and Gentile, whether they reciprocated it or not. He loved those who beat, jailed, and falsely accused him. He devoted his life to the passion of Christ – *nothing else mattered.*

Some scientists attribute his vision and dramatic transformation to either a mood disorder or psychosis. *I need that psychosis.* I need the disorder that gives me love, joy, peace, patience, kindness, goodness, faithfulness, gentleness, and self-control. I need the disorder that transforms my world with love.

Atheists, agnostics, and Comfortable Christians have something in common. We have no desire to seek the true Jesus. And seeking Jesus isn't just about finding the light; it's about *becoming the light.*

What is light?

I'll tell you what it's not. People are sick of the impractical, merely emotional, culturally traditional, fear-based faith in Jesus. Many of us who barely manage to cling to the faith are waning. We have lost the passion and purpose of seeking Christ. Perhaps we too, have never *truly* encountered Him.

ATHEISTS & CHRISTIANS UNITE:
A proposal

Dear angry *angry* atheists,

I've noticed that virtually every news article or social media post regarding a faith-based issue is accompanied with angry atheist comments. I find your hate for Christianity to be surprising. Why not just be indifferent to God, like us Comfortable Christians.

Now, we could discuss our differences all day — you all believe the world's wars are due to religion, when they're clearly due to science. Lord willing, we would've eradicated science — *perhaps with holy crusade!*

But let's be diplomatic.

You see, we have a lot in common. Both of us live everyday — with the exception of Sunday — exactly the same. We completely understand when you say, "I don't need God." *We agree!* (Though, not in words, of course).

In addition, both of us seek to fulfill our carnal desires. In fact, *we pray for them!* We've even gone as far as extending our materialistic approach to the afterlife. Personally, I can't wait 'til King Jesus hands me the keys to my very own 'Thugs Mansion' in Benevolence Hills!

Another similarity shared is that neither of us depends on the Bible as if it were daily bread. In fact, you atheists may read it more than we do! Granted, it's for the purpose of debate.

Furthermore, we both consider ourselves to be good people, generally speaking. We've come to this conclusion because we aren't *physically* harming others — neglecting the harm we cause when we operate by the lust of our flesh, the lust for materials, and our pride.

This vague sentiment of personal goodness enables us to judge others as bad. It creates within us a self-righteous sentiment—we're good without God.

Not to mention, we're just as closed-minded! Your worldview has become as intolerant and proselytizing as the religions you all oppose.

We're in a bit of a *stalemate*, in reference to both our gridlock against each other and our inability to remain monogamous. *Once again,* carnal desires. The old adage rings true, "If you can't beat 'em, join 'em." After all, the only substantial difference between you guys and us is that while you have chosen to deny Christ in word, we do it in deed. The core of our seemingly contrasted worldview is *merely* our approach. We cling to traditional faith, yet render it void.

Different approach, *same result!*

This is precisely why I am extending to you, angry atheists, an olive branch. There's no need to defy us; *we defy ourselves!* The contradiction within us goes against God while professing God. *We're your greatest allies.* Ultimately, Comfortable Christianity is more threatening to theism than your science.

Don't try to reason with us; we *are not* reasonable people. We don't even act on what we believe. If we did, I suspect that we wouldn't be so angrily pitted against you. After all, Jesus said that the 'whole law' is to love God and love your neighbor.

Surely you wouldn't hate us Christians too much if we *accurately* represented Christ. We would essentially 'kill you with kindness' — now that the *Separation of Church and State* bars us from, *you know,* just killing you.

But before we — atheists and Christians — agree to disagree, before we unite and skip together into the horizon, I would like to reconcile the issue that caused me to write this: your angry, offensive posts.

I used to wonder if the website administrators should just wipe out your clearly destructive comments. They ruin the constructive purpose of having a comment section. But of course, an intervention would be deemed as censorship. It would impede your 'free speech' in a similar manner in which an intervention by the universe's Administrator would impede your 'free will.' In addition, this censorship would create a site where only those who agree with the administrator would be tolerated.

This is good news, because we both — Comfortable Christians and atheists — oppose God. *Yet He tolerates us,* for now. Ultimately, God's existence is a detriment to us all. *We're in this together,* my friends. We are the unlikeliest of allies.

So here's my proposal: If you can get by our falsehood, we can get by your disbelief. Let's bury the hatchet. Perhaps we can go to a bar? *The first round is on me.* After all, I've been stacking mucho dinero by arriving at church *after* the collection of tithes and offering!

Sincerely,

The Comfort Counselor

I DREAM OF JESUS

In big cities, the homeless are at every corner. Their squalor either evokes our compassion or apathy. If we offer them food, we'll find that some will refuse.

On one particular occasion, a 'hungry' man approached me as I exited a pizzeria. I offered him my carryout, which he opened and handed back, vocalizing his disgust with my choice of topping. *Pepperoni.*

It was clear that he would prefer cash, to use at his own discretion. However, the discretion of a homeless man is questionable. In fact, his current living conditions, or the lack thereof, may itself be a consequence of successive lapses of discretion. Some, not all, may claim to be hungry, but truthfully, they want to buy drugs and alcohol.

 Have you ever wanted to witness to the homeless, but were afraid of them? *Don't risk contracting diseases!* Just tape a Bible verse to a can of beans and roll it in their direction. Once you've retreated to a safe distance, grab a pair of binoculars and watch them give their lives to Jesus.

Many Christians operate like homeless beggars. We're not seeking refuge, strength, and sustenance in Christ. Instead, we're often seeking miracles at our discretion. But often, our discretion is questionable.

"When you ask, you do not receive, because you ask with wrong motives, that you may spend what you get on your pleasures." James 4:3

NO CO-SIGN

We often find ourselves making bull-crap prayers. There are three major types: 1) We need a miracle, 2) We need something outside of God's will, and 3) the verbatim prayer, done out of habit.

TYPE #1

We need a miracle! This prayer is usually made in lieu of being responsible. It could be anything from: a) passing a test we haven't studied for, b) healing a menacing hangover, or c) not being pregnant.

In exchange for God's services, we promise to never be in this situation again. *We find ourselves in this situation again.* Why not be genuine to God? His role in our lives is a clean-up guy, a divine butler! And our payment to Him is empty promises.

TYPE #2.

This prayer contradicts God's will. It can be anything from: a) Lord, make me so rich that I don't have to depend on you, to b) Lord, please pour out your wrath upon all the Muslims, homosexuals, atheists (generally anyone to whom you have called me to be a light).

The tragedy in these prayers is that we end them with "in Jesus's name." *Jesus ain't co-signing that bull-crap!* We give God a laundry list of things to do without first examining our prayers. In fact, when we say "in Jesus's name," we're saying that our request is in line with Jesus's will.

We're forging Christ's signature. It might be better to recognize whose will we're actually seeking to fulfill – *our own.* To put things into context, let's use our own names at the end of the prayer.

TYPE #3.

This prayer is often said verbatim. The problem is that we're praying it out of habit and not from our hearts. I often catch myself doing this type of prayer for my meals – if somehow I remembered and am willing to expose myself in the midst of onlookers. (Oftentimes that onlooker is my atheist dog – *she never prays*). My prayer goes, "Lord, thank you for this day. Thank you for this food. In Jesus's name. Amen." *Bull-crap!*

 To avoid getting funny looks when you say grace, use the drive-thru first and then walk in. There's a blind spot in between the pay window and the pick-up window where no one can see you.

THE MAGIC LAMP

"And I will do whatever you ask in my name, so that the Father may be glorified by the Son." John 14:13

Growing up, my friends and I used to fantasize about *Aladdin* and *I Dream of Jeannie*. We would ask ourselves, "What would you wish for?" There were the usual responses: toys, pizza, and toys made of pizza. I fancied myself a bit smarter, reserving my last wish to be *unlimited wishes!*

In my mind, I would have outsmarted the genie. This all-powerful being would now be my servant! I would speak things into existence, naming and claiming them, *hallelujah!*

We're all grown up now, and sadly, yet to find a genie. We figure Jesus will just have to do as we convert all of our wishes into prayers. We haven't lost that same self-centered imagination. After all, He "will do whatever" we ask in His name. *Rub the Bible and make three wishes!*

If Jesus appeared before you and granted you wishes, what would you ask for? Money, status, a relationship? What would you ask for if you could make an all-powerful being your servant? In *Aladdin*, Jafar wished to become the genie. Perhaps that's what we want, to become God.

Our prayers often oppose the very point of making them — "so that the Father may be glorified by the Son." Before we ask Him to do our bidding, to go against His own will, or just blabber the same disingenuous prayer, let's examine what exactly we're saying.

Our prayers are a reflection of what we want out of God.

TO PRAY OR NOT TO PRAY

I've always struggled to consistently devote even a morsel of time to my Lord and Savior. Sure, there have been periods when my prayer life was strong — you know, the hours following a revival conference. Otherwise, I've either struggled to stay committed, or I've given up trying.

I've silently wondered why I have so many excuses. It's always something. "I'm in a rush," or, "I'm too busy," or, "I'm too tired."

I began to see that my relationship with Jesus was purely selfish. My interest isn't in surrendering my day to Him; it's enhancing my day through Him. He is something I go through with the aim of achieving a good day or a good result. Jesus has been demoted from Savior to personal assistant. He has become the mediator between goal and man, not God and man.

My prayer is usually in regards to reaching a point where I no longer struggle, in the material sense. Whether it be finances, finances, or even finances — I want Jesus to help me get to a place where I will be so comfortable (with finances) that I won't need to pray. *Essentially.*

If my days have been relatively good — my goals within reach — do I need to go through Jesus? *No.* Prayer time had become an enhancement, not a surrender. It was contingent on me needing something as opposed to me surrendering something.

Surrender is what I fear.

I think of all the things I'm not willing to give up. *I avoid prayer to avoid surrender.* And if I must pray — given that I'm in a bind of some sort — it's accompanied with a promise of surrender. It's as if I feel that I must incentivize my supplication; my prayer is a bribe. For example, if I was feeling sick after a night of partying, I'd promise that God I'd never drink again. *Who am I fooling?*

Obviously, King Jesus can't be bribed. So my aim in making these promises was to bribe myself. The purpose of prayer is to submit, to surrender. But since I'm not willing to do that freely, I must persuade myself to be bribed under my own conditions, granted that Jesus performs. If not, He has breached the contract and I will recoup any losses I had surrendered in advance!

Herein lies the problem. The first thing that must be surrendered is my pride. I can't obey my Lord unless I submit to His lordship in my life. The very things I fear I may have to surrender, are only secondary. It's as if I'm promising God I will run, without learning how to walk.

He knows I can't fulfill my promise. I know I'm not truly willing. Yet the question remains: to pray or not to pray?

THE LORD'S PRAYER

"This, then, is how you should pray: Our Father in heaven, hallowed be your name, your kingdom come, your will be done, on earth as it is in heaven. Give us this today our daily bread. And forgive us our debts, as we also have forgiven our debtors. And lead us not into temptation, but deliver us from the evil one." Matthew 6:9-13

This is the type of prayer Jesus taught us to pray:
1. Acknowledge our Source, and pray for His kingdom to come. We oftentimes miss that His kingdom isn't something that is physical, but something meant to be in our midst (Luke 17:20-21).
2. Pray for God's will, not our own. We often distort the meaning of prayer with our self-centered wishes.
3. Ask for our daily bread – His word and guidance, *not a McRib sandwich.*
4. Ask for the forgiveness of our sins and the strength to forgive those who have sinned against us.
5. Pray for deliverance from temptation and evil.

What kind of genie is this? He makes you ask for stuff *He* wants!

Many non-believers say they like Jesus; they just don't like His fan club. But there are two distinct groups within what they refer to as 'His fan club'. The type of prayer we direct towards Jesus identifies whether we're the paparazzi or the entourage.

PAPARAZZI VS. ENTOURAGE

"Jesus answered, 'Very truly I tell you, you are looking for me… because you ate the loaves and had your fill.'" John 6:26

Jesus was and is a celebrity. Celebrities usually have two main groups surrounding them: the paparazzi and the entourage. Both groups have distinct intentions.

One of the greatest nuisances for celebrities is the paparazzi. The paparazzi pester them everywhere they go. Their aim is to extract information, photos, and stories for gossip media outlets. Essentially, they're not chasing the celebrity; they're chasing the celebrity's status. They get as close as possible to derive something. They should never be confused as friends.

On the other hand, the entourage is comprised of true friends. They can be trusted because they're of kindred spirit. They aren't there for celebrity status; they're there for friendship.

"The knowledge of the secrets of the kingdom of heaven have been given to you, but not them." Matthew 13:11

When we read the word 'you,' we often plug in our names. We appropriate God's promises – everything from prospering to being highly favored. Name it; claim it. Believe it; receive it.

But what if Jesus was referring to us as 'them' and not as 'you'? After all, He was speaking to the masses that followed Him, but the understanding was only for His entourage.

Are we 'you' or 'them'? Are we in the crowd around Jesus, or truly *with* Him? Are we the paparazzi or the entourage? One way we can know for sure is by looking at our intentions.

For the crowd, going to see Jesus must have been a cool thing to do. They had witnessed some miracles, heard a good sermon, and if they were lucky, eaten a miraculous Filet-O-Fish sandwich. The crowds were hoping to get something from Jesus, but the disciples were extensions of Him.

We often think of God's kingdom as a means to expand our own. Our hope in Jesus is often a pipe dream of Jesus. Do we value Christ or value what we may be able to get out of Him? (You know, since He's all-powerful).

So many claim they're hungry for Jesus. But all they want is material. Just like the homeless guy who rejected my dinner, they reject the real Jesus. Are we seeking Him, to be like Him, or are we seeking miracles? When we objectify God, when our trust in Him is for the material life, chances are, He will let us down.

GOD IS GOOD, SOMETIMES

When something good happens–whether we worked for it or it just worked out, we like to attribute it to God's goodness. For example, "I got the job! God is good!" But if we were qualified, worked hard, and interviewed well, perhaps God didn't need to overcompensate with His goodness. *Perhaps we are good!* Even if we weren't, it could have been a bit of luck.

I used to struggle trying to differentiate between what was coincidence and what was actually God miraculously moving in my favor. It didn't help that Christians often credited frivolous things as an example of God's goodness. It seemed that everything – from getting good parking to buying the last coffee cake at Starbucks – constituted giving glory to God.

Now, there's nothing wrong with giving God glory for everything (in fact, this is our purpose as Christians). But we seem more eager give glory to God when we're getting things. It fits our definition of 'favor' and 'good'. We glorify God when He glorifies us.

Did God save you that parking space so you didn't have to walk? Did He really protect your coffee cake, perhaps blinding irreligious customers from its existence? *Shoot*, an atheist may have missed the entire store's existence! I shook my head at these religious nuts who said such things. What about the Christians in Africa who are starving? Is God still good? After all, He didn't save them coffee cake!

 Think 'Africa' and not downtown to make it feel like the needy are too far to help.

After years of deliberation, I finally conceded that thanking God, whether good things were coincidence or not, wouldn't hurt. *It was a positive mindset.* Yeah, that's it. After all, if I robbed God of the glory, He may not *perform* for me again.

The problem isn't failing to thank God when things are good, but failing to thank God when things are bad. Rarely do Christians say, "I didn't get the job. God is good!" Giving praise when things don't go our way – now *that* is special. And potentially annoying.

Christians often respond to the casual question, "How are you?" with "I'm blessed." What does that mean? Well, it can mean anything from "good things are happening" to "I have no major gripes." But what if bad things are happening? Based on how we've been assessing the fruit of God's goodness, He's only good sometimes.

THE SCRAPS THAT REMAIN

While moving, I came across an old scrapbook I had written in over 10 years ago. I spent the next couple hours examining old doodles, poems, and never-published rap lyrics. I was examining the 19-year-old me who believed he was going to make a splash in the non-existent Gospel-gangster rap music industry. I chuckled while reading my old lyrics, which were heavily based on violently murdering the devil.

Then I came across some sobering material. At the time, I was confused about the meaning of my life, which I expressed in poorly doodled self-portraits that replaced my facial features with huge question marks. At 19 years of age, I felt hopeless – my mind relentlessly polluted with suicidal thoughts. I didn't want to exist. I couldn't find my purpose.

To make things worse, I had lost my older brother to cancer. Pain and depression rippled through the writings. As I read, I became overwhelmed with emotion, reliving the loss. *It was like he died all over again.* Clutching a scrapbook that I had forgotten existed, I cried. Teardrops hadn't hit those pages for a decade.

I believed in God, but was He really good? After all, He didn't answer my family's prayers for healing. He allowed my brother – a husband and father – to die. A once strong man, he had shriveled before my eyes. What's the use in serving a God that doesn't heal His people? What's the use in a God that allows us to suffer?

As my brother edged closer to death, I quit praying from him. I figured I was wasting my breath. Simultaneously, I grew disconnected from the family, and disconnected from him, as he was dying. His last words to me were, "I am disappointed in you."

It still pierces through me.

As the pages continued, I began to see a time when I re-connected with a childhood friend who was going through a similar situation. Her father had beaten cancer the first time, but it came back – just the way it had for my brother. We bonded on the premise of pain.

As our friendship turned into romance, my self-worth, happiness, and purpose were restored – *she became my purpose.* I began to excel in college, going from a 2.5 GPA to a 3.4. My life had new meaning… for a few years. When the relationship end-ed, I found myself in a *greater depression* than the first one.

In the midst of reading the book, my jaw dropped. I had never before made the correlation between the two greatest mo-ments of depression in my life. The source of my hurt at 19 was the same at 22 – a sense of meaninglessness. My loss of purpose had re-emerged because I never resolved it; *I numbed it.* I put my faith in something perishable, and I was perishing with it.

Depression was back with a fury. I blamed her when I should have blamed myself. Theoretically, my joy, peace, and purpose should never have depended on someone other than Jesus. *Theoretically*. But I was mad at Him for my brother's death. My days were swept away in vice; I didn't want to hurt.

Those old suicidal thoughts came back. I was tired. Between my job at TSA and school, I barely slept. I remember driving on the 405 freeway to work at 5 a.m. thinking, *just crash*. You need a break, even if it's permanent!

This is the moment where you may expect me to say I turned to Jesus and He gave me peace. *No.* I continued, got over it, and found purpose in something else.

If you have ever endured pain, you may have noticed how well you can connect with someone with similar hurt. Many nonprofits begin by making this same connection. Oftentimes, their loved ones were affected by disease, gun violence, or some senseless act. Their suffering is relieved by connecting to strangers with the same suffering.

THE PREMISE OF PAIN

A year ago, I was reading an article about Ethiopian, Eritrean, and Sudanese refugees who were traveling to Israel to seek asylum. The person being interviewed had lived to tell his story of being captured by human traffickers. Men, women, and children were beaten, raped, sold or killed. We usually turn a blind eye to these horrifying stories because there's nothing we can do, we think. But this particular one hit me hard, since I am a child of parents who successfully emigrated from that region.

Is God still good when you're dying young, or violently? Is He good when you're being human trafficked? Is God still good when you're being raped? Would you still respond, "I'm blessed," when asked how you're doing? We often praise God in happiness, but we may curse Him in pain. *Where is our 'good' God now?*

The survivor – who had endured seven months of torture – told the interviewer that if he came across another victim of this evil, to tell this person, "May the strength of Job be with you." (jhsph.edu) Never in a million years did I think someone could derive anything positive from Job's life. But this man, who had suffered so much, connected with Job on the premise of pain.

THE GOOD SUFFER

Very few stories are more perplexing than the miserable life of Job. God allowed the devil to take his wealth, health, and children. All for what — *to prove his loyalty?*

My understanding from Sunday School was that since Job was ultimately restored and had more kids later, it all worked out! *What!?!* You can't replace family! "It worked out" didn't help me understand why a 'good' God would allow a good person to suffer so much.

"Naked I came from my mother's womb, and naked I will depart. The Lord gave and the Lord has taken away; may the name of the Lord be praised." Job 1:21

Somehow, he gave glory to God in his darkest moments. His wife advised him, "Are you still maintaining your integrity? Curse God and die!" He replied, "Shall we accept good from God, and not trouble?" (Job 2:9-10)

What use is God if He can't keep us from trouble? We depend on Him to live cushy lives where there's no suffering, where there's no loss, where there is no pain. *It's our American Dream!* We want Him to spare us the agony that His own Son was not spared so we can praise Him for good parking.

We depend on Christ to keep us comfortable – ever failing to realize that He too felt forsaken. Our love and faith in Him is fickle if it depends on whether we *feel* like He's there.

THE FORSAKEN KING

"My God, my God, why have you forsaken me? Why are you so far from saving me, so far from my cries of anguish?" Psalm 22:1

Jesus recited this psalm when He was crucified. A bad thing happened to a good man – a man with no sin. Even Jesus struggled to find any strength, to the point where He sweat blood. When God has seemingly forsaken us, we oftentimes forsake Him back.

Jesus claimed to give us life, and life more abundantly! *But He suffered and died!* Either He's a lunatic who offers nothing, or the life He's referring to is born through suffering and death — which still makes Him sound like a lunatic. The manner in which He died was so horrific that the early Christians didn't use the cross as a symbol. *But we can,* because we're completely disconnected with its meaning – *suffering and death.*

Even Christ's birth was accompanied by suffering. King Herod commanded the slaughter of babies when he learned of prophecy that a king was born in Bethlehem. Jesus's family escaped to Egypt, but imagine being a parent who did not. Imagine the bitterness of burying your baby. *Where is your 'good' God?*

My God suffered. I can't believe in a God that didn't, one that didn't suffer like His children – *one that can't relate to His children.* In Jesus, I seek life through the suffering, not life without it.

In college, I took a humanities course. I loved learning about the different religions, and I aced all the exams – except the one on Christianity. I managed a 'C-'. I thought I knew it, so I didn't bother studying. I was more interested in Buddhism – the first of the *Four Noble Truths* being that "life is suffering." I could relate.

As much as I could relate to suffering, Christ could relate so much more. If it weren't for Jesus, my faith in a Creator may still seem possible, but His benevolence would be in serious question. He would have created an environment that He wasn't willing to be subject to. What makes seeking Christ unique is that He's not just God, but He understands our pain. *He can relate.* That's what makes it possible for me to believe His words: "I am in the Father and the Father is in me" (John 14:11).

Suffering can either lead us away from or to the cross. We either reject Jesus for not preventing pain, or we identify with His. Just as the trafficking survivor found strength in Job, we can find strength in the cross, placing our hope in something that although is intangible, *is imperishable.*

THE PRESERVATIVE OF THE MASSES

We can put our faith in something perishable, or in the Imperishable. What we can't do is place our faith in the Imperishable *to keep the perishable.* But we still try. Oftentimes, our trust in God is *to preserve our comfort.* And when that's shaken, so is our faith. God is good because He is hope, not because He gives good parking, a good job, or a good meal.

If we're defining Him by how He preserves the perishable – the material life and purpose – then He's only good sometimes. Depending on our situation, *He may be evil!* 'Casting our cares on Jesus' isn't always about protecting our cares. It may be about having the strength to push through.

God is good because *God is hope.* Without a creator, we're just evolved animals, trying to socially construct what good, hope, and purpose are – all of which become relative. The human definition of them always changes. If there's no God, there's no true definition; it's your truth versus my truth.

"For as I walked around and looked carefully at your objects of worship, I even found an altar with this inscription: TO AN UNKNOWN GOD. So you are ignorant of the very thing you worship—and this is what I am going to proclaim to you." Acts 17:23

Before monotheism became the powerhouse it is today, there were many other popular theories and 'isms.' When Paul went to Athens – a place where thinkers from around the world did nothing but discuss Polytheism, Gnosticism, and other beliefs – he introduced to them the concept of one God, Christ the Redeemer. Some sneered; some were interested.

To the Athenians, it wasn't a matter of 'is there a God' or not; to them, there were many gods. Ultimately, all of the gods have all failed. We've trimmed the number down to one God, who is in control of everything – yet still manages to fail us (in regards to preserving the perishable). This causes many to say, "There's no God."

We've all thought, "If I were God, I would do this, I would do that." *Oh, if only we could vote on what God should do.* The debate has changed from *God vs. gods*, to *God vs. no-God* – which ultimately makes me, by default, my own god. *God vs. a no-God god!*

"The life of mortals is like grass, they flourish like a flower of the field; the wind blows over is and it is gone, and its place remembers it no more. But from everlasting to everlasting the Lord's love is with those who fear him." Psalms 103:16-17

The problem is, we're in love with perishable things. We derive our happiness from them. We can all agree that our happiness comes from family, friends, wealth, hobbies – whatever it is we enjoy. *They are the source of our purpose.* And if or when they perish, so do we.

What do we have left when a loved one dies, a relationship ends, or all our money is gone? What happens when the things we depend on to give us purpose, perish?

All we have left is the hope that we once forsook, the hope that Jesus makes sense of this chaos. The hope that there's something more to life than perishable things – *that there is life after suffering and death.*

THE ANGEL OF LIGHT

The catch is, we're not going to come to Him when things are fine. We come when our worlds are falling apart, either to pray, "God, get me out of this," or "God, why did you allow this?"

The devil has no interest in driving you towards God. I read a meme that depicted the cliché devil – red skin and horns – telling a crying woman, "Your life is terrible!" But on the other side of her was Jesus – looking all beautiful and saying, "Just focus on me, baby."

Well, He didn't say 'baby,' but you get the point: when things are rough, look to Jesus. After all, we connect with Him through His suffering and death, right? But the thing is, Satan *is* beautiful – he comes as an angel of light! He's far more appealing than Jesus, despite how smoking hot Hollywood may depict Him.

The devil isn't going to make you cry so you can run to Jesus. Unless, of course, you're going to tell Jesus that you hate Him. Instead, the devil will say, "Your life isn't that bad; you're a good person. You don't hurt anybody."

The popular gauge today whether someone is good is if they hurt others or not. They say, "I can do what I want as long as I don't hurt people." (It is unclear whether they mean this in the physical sense, or emotionally as well. And of course, 'justified hurt,' as in retaliation, is exempt.) Ultimately, they may be hurting themselves, as I have. Even as Christians, we place our faith in perishable things: relationships, wealth, and health. *Our faith may fail.*

"Come to me, all you who are weary and burdened, and I will give you rest. Take my yoke upon you and learn from me, for I am gentle and humble in heart, and you will find rest for your souls." Matthew 11:28-29

If we're gauging God's benevolence on pain and suffering, He's only good sometimes. What makes God good is that He represents hope through suffering, by suffering Himself. *He is hope beyond the perishable.* Jesus calls those who are suffering to Him; He identifies with them.

My impression of Christ is this: He is hope beyond this selfish, meaningless, painful, insatiable, chaotic existence – an existence driven to numb ourselves with substances. Does this concede that I am weak, weary, and burdened? *So be it.* With a dose of humility, I choose to learn from Jesus. In Him I *hope* to find rest for my soul.

"I am not asking anyone to accept Christianity if his best reasoning tells him that the weight of the evidence is against it. That is not the point at which faith comes in." -C.S. Lewis

PART 2:
LOST IN TRANSFIGURATION

MERLOT OR MEDICINE:
A reintroduction

Like many people, I enjoy an occasional nightcap. But on one particular night, I had a blistering headache – *I needed medicine.* Yet, I shamelessly attempted to persuade myself that Merlot was medicine.

The internal debate made my migraine worsen.

I popped a few ibuprofen pills and dove onto my bed, face-first. A short while later, I abruptly awoke, sweating profusely. Well, I don't actually sweat; I glisten. *I was glistening profusely.* So I got up and turned on the A/C.

That's when I realized my headache was gone. *Nice!* Briefly charmed, I crawled back into bed. That's when I realized I was wide awake. *Crap!*

Then I thought, "Hey, I should have that Merlot to help me feel sleepy." That's when I remembered, mixing ibuprofen and alcohol can cause stomach bleeding. *Crap!* It was an uncomfortable truth – a truth I wished I was ignorant of.

But would one glass hurt?

I decided to consult a medical professional, a.k.a. Google search. At first, I was only interested in seemingly credible sites like *Web M.D.* However, it insisted that I'd already suffered internal bleeding and a list of other potentially fatal ailments. It stopped short of giving me the number of hours I had left to live and redirecting me to a Notary Public to sign my Last Will and Testament.

I just wanted Merlot!

A bit rattled, I continued my search. I couldn't find information that supported my desire to drink after taking medicine. I was looking for something that backed my inclination, perhaps something that read, "Wine and ibuprofen? Yeah that's cool!"

I began looking at less credible forums and random blogs. I even ventured deep into the "No Man's Land" of the Internet——pages 3 and 4 of Google search. It's a place one only goes in a state of desperation.

I was in a state of desperation, never stopping to think about why I needed this 'occasional' nightcap.

"Why not pray?" I suggested. *"Why not shut up?"* I suggested.

And that's when I finally found it. The confirmation I had been searching for read, "Wine and ibuprofen? Yeah that's cool!"

Yes! Yes! Yes!

Thank you so much username 'dirtbag2001'. Another advocate, username 'slimNshady15', chimed in. His message claimed, "I actually wash down the ibuprofen with vodka!"

Wait a minute! This is, oh no... it's sarcasm! *Crap!*

In that moment, I learned something about myself. I had no interest in the truth. My interest was only in finding something that would make me feel confident and comfortable with what I wanted to be true.

We all want information that supports our interests, whether personal or corporate. We hope to find data that backs what we want to believe, what we want to project, and we overlook what we object. It defies reason to keep intact the sentiment, "What I am doing is right, or good... or okay."

This is precisely why there is so much contradiction amongst Christians. We're all seeking information about Jesus that would suit our own interests and lifestyles. Essentially, we begin to create our own imaginary Jesus.

My Jesus understands that I don't have time for Him. *My Jesus* is okay with this, or hates that. *My Jesus* only loves who I love; He is indifferent to those I am indifferent to. Rarely does *my Jesus* demand discipline.

In essence, *my Jesus* is a figment of *my imagination.*

We love to settle our contradictions by saying, "God knows my heart." I've come to the realization that this cliché is not the least bit soothing. *Why?* Because the more I search my heart, the more darkness I find. My heart's desire is to serve itself, even when serving others – even when serving God.

Instead of representing Jesus, our Jesus represents us.

Ultimately we turn from Him, the true Him, for an imaginary version. We go a step further and find pastors that make the same modifications. But it won't be as blatant as 'username: falseprophet666.' Ultimately, our imaginary Jesus won't disturb our comfort.

What we don't see is the internal bleeding – the destruction that begins on the inside and works its way out.

"We have all departed from that total plan in different ways, and each of us wants to make out that his own modification of the original plan is the plan itself. You will find this again and again about anything that is really Christian: every one is attracted by bits of it and wants to pick out those bits and leave the rest. That is why we do not get much further: and that is why people who are fighting for

quite opposite things can both say they are fighting for Christianity." -
C. S. Lewis

AMBIGUOUS ALMIGHTY

As a child, I noticed all the different types of Jesuses: white Jesus, Asian Jesus, and even (what some may call a sacrilegious) *black Jesus*. I understand the desire to make Him relate to all people, but where will His racial ambiguity end? Eskimo Jesus? Aborigine Jesus? Perhaps Samoan Jesus?

 **Tip** You may compromise on many things, but refuse to do so when it comes to your faith in Jesus's race. Who dares to deny that our dear Lord has angelic blond hair and piercing blue eyes? Who dares to blaspheme the inspired, inerrant, infallible depiction by Michelangelo?!

Most of us are not eagerly anticipating the Second Coming to settle this racial dispute. (But then again, most of us are not eagerly anticipating the Second Coming to begin with). Until then, we can all agree that Jesus was tall, strong, and devilishly handsome. These are all attributes in which we find worth, and we'd want to see the King of kings embody.

"Do not look at his appearance or at the height of his stature, because I have rejected him; for God sees not as man sees, for man looks at the outward appearance, but the LORD looks at the heart." 1 Samuel 16:7

The physical misrepresentation of Jesus is trivial compared to the ideological misrepresentation. Not only have we tried to identify Jesus with our race, we want Him to champion our beliefs.

Christian or not, we all make something of Jesus. He was capitalist or socialist, merciful or wrathful, humble or majestic, prophet or messiah. He has been used to control the masses, to save the masses, to judge the masses. Some think of Him as *one* of the ways to God; some think of Him when they need stuff from God.

As Christians, we've failed to accurately represent Christ's ideology. Instead, we've made Him represent our ideology. If we're living in sin, *He's forgiving.* If we're living for materials, *He wants to us to prosper.* If we boast in our good deeds, *He casts the first stone.* We've made it so difficult for people to see Jesus's heart.

MAN IN THE MIRROR

Our misrepresentation of Christ has turned away millions, if not billions of people. My hope is that non-believers would be able to push aside Christians to see Christ. And I'll begin with the man in the mirror.

Perhaps by examining my own hypocrisy, I can encourage others to do the same: Not to merely accept ourselves as frauds, but to be transfigured into what Christ has called us to be – *a light to the world.*

As I consider how many people I've known, I wonder, *how many of them have I led to Christ?* How many have I led away? I like to think I've had neutral influence, but there's no such thing. If my friends, neighbors, and co-workers know that I'm a Christian, they will examine my life – *even if I don't.*

Perhaps it would be better if they didn't know.

SKELETON IN THE CLOSET

Christian teens and young adults are often encouraged to witness to friends. But the thought can be daunting, especially since revealing that we're Christians may come as a shocking surprise.

Surely being a follower of Jesus isn't something that can fly under the radar. After all, we're 'not of this world,' remember? They should be able to distinguish us from the general population, just as we can spot a foreigner a *kilometer* away.

Kilometer, *hah*. I crack myself up.

Oftentimes, our language, behavior, and entire lives are no different from the people we seek to minister to. Despite this discrepancy, we may still manage to witness when we've mustered up the courage. *Liquid courage!*

People love being social, especially with the aid of substances. Many of us Christians seamlessly join them. And since being inebriated facilitates an open, no reservations zone, some of us have found ourselves opening up about our faith.

Just as tipsy people blabber meaningless nonsense, "I love you man, (barf)" our testimony is meaningless nonsense. A slurred testimony, a high testimony, or any testimony that allows us to make the disclaimer that, although we're not living right, we know the truth – *it just hasn't set us free yet.*

Our verbal testimonies are being nullified by our compromising lives. A non-believing friend of mine once laughingly told me about how his Christian girlfriend felt guilty about their sexual relationship. *OUCH!* Her ability to witness to him was dead.

"You are the salt of the earth. But if the salt loses saltiness, how can it be made salty again? It is no longer good for anything, except to be thrown out and trampled underfoot." Matthew 5:13

When we live compromising lives, no one can tell that we have faith in Christ. In fact, if we tell them, we may be disfiguring the image of Christ. We may have become the salt that has lost its saltiness – void of taste and the ability to create thirst.

Does this mean we shouldn't witness because our lives aren't holy enough? We're all a 'work in progress,' until of course, *we stop making progress.* Faith without works is dead, and sharing it is just exposing the skeleton in the closet.

PLATFORM POLITICS

"First off, I'd like to thank God for changing my life – letting me realize what life is all about. Basketball is just a platform." –Kevin Durant

For Christians, few things are more inspiring than watching a celebrity believer give glory to God on television: not some faith-based network, but on *ESPN!* On this platform, *the whole world is watching!*

But rarely do we realize that any position, regardless of accolade, *is a platform.* Whether we're great or small, public figures or average Joes, we need to 'realize what life is all about.' Anyone can say, "glory to God," but what's incredible is making non-believers give glory to God – *without the threat of violence.*

"Let your light shine before men in such a way that they may see your good works, and glorify your Father who is in heaven." Matthew 5:16

Bringing glory to God is something we can do at any position. From the CEO to the janitor, we're all encouraged to do our work unto the Lord. (Colossians 3:23) Our testimony is strengthened when people can see our integrity and weakened when they see the lack of it.

Picture yourself as an unbeliever who is hearing the Gospel from a lazy co-worker, a gossiping co-worker, or even a stole-your-lunch-from-the-breakroom-fridge co-worker. This person's public association with Christ is actually a detriment! When we fail to strive for excellence in faith, work, and integrity, our lives become a platform that *takes* away glory from God.

MY KINGDOM COME

Oftentimes, we try to bribe God into giving us a greater platform. If He would just expand our territory, give us a higher position, or a stage, then we would use it to glorify Him! Never mind that our current platform is bringing Him shame. A greater platform would only serve to bring Him greater shame. It's less about God, and more about us. Jesus is just a tool, a platform for our glory.

Throughout history, people have used God to push their agendas – whether it was a militant conquest, an appeal to a political base, or simply personal ambition. It all began with the misunderstanding that the King of the Jews would star in a revolution that would restore Israel's former glory. Even Jesus's disciples expected Him to bring a kingdom, and they sought to be seated on His right and left side.

"The coming of the kingdom of God is not something that can be observed, nor will people say, 'Here it is,' or 'There it is,' because the kingdom of God is in your midst." Luke 17:20-21

Jesus was not the king that would overthrow the Romans. To their dismay, He was the king that would overthrow the temple! He was angered by how the house of the Lord had been turned into a business. People were profiting on God! *Sound familiar?* So he made a whip of cords and drove everyone out, shouting, "My house will be called a house of prayer, but you are making it a den of robbers" (Matthew 21:13).

The Jewish leaders were angry. They had been using God as a platform to support their self-righteousness, status, and profit. Jesus's healing power, revolutionary teaching, and popularity threatened them. They hated Him and His mission. Nowadays, we idealize Him, but not His mission. *Does that make us any better?*

Actually, it may make us worse. After all, we've disfigured His purpose. When we *use* Jesus to endorse our goals, it exhibits that we don't really want Him — we want Barabbas!

"They shouted back, 'No, not him! Give us Barabbas!' Now Barabbas had taken part in an uprising." John 18:40

Pilate offered a prisoner to be freed — either Jesus or Barabbas. Barabbas was a symbol of Israel's zealot platform; he revolted against Rome. Unlike Jesus, he didn't condemn their religious hypocrisy and profiteering.

Have you ever wondered if you prefer Jesus or Barabbas?

THE MOUNT OF DISFIGURATION

When Jesus appeared with Moses and Elijah, His face shone like the sun, His clothes became bright. He was glorified before them, and a voice from the clouds said, "This is my Son, whom I love; with him I am well pleased" (Matthew 17:5). The disciples witnessed the transfiguration of Christ, but we have witnessed the disfiguration. It isn't being perpetrated by the outspoken enemies of God, but by us, Comfortable Christians — sons and daughters in whom He is not well pleased.

If we don't consider our lives to be a platform to glorify Jesus, then Jesus is just a platform to glorify our lives. Christianity has been broken up into pieces of greed, self-righteousness, status, political power, and hypocrisy — *everything Jesus was against.* Ultimately, our platform has taken away glory from God. And look, *the whole world is watching!*

JESUS PIECE

"I'm far from religious but I got beliefs, so I put canary yellow diamonds in my Jesus piece" - The Game

Jesus Piece: a charm necklace of either a crucifix or the likeness of Jesus, sometimes but not always studded with jewels.

Rap videos have it all: cars, girls, and Jesus pieces. Surprisingly, rappers are not the holiest of people. But who are we to judge? They still 'shout out' to the Lord and brandish iced-out Jesus pieces. *Praise Him!* They deserve an ovation. Somehow, they have made time to represent their faith in between the weed smoke, the strippers, and the weed-smoking strippers. And when they win the music award for the song, 'Weed Smoke & Strippers in the VIP,' they won't fail to give glory to God.

No! We're not ashamed! We love shoutin' out Jesus. In fact, many of us have cross necklaces and tattoos. Jesus may not be visible by our lives, but He *sure as hell* will be by our jewelry! You'd think God would appreciate this gesture of 'good faith,' but somehow He's more concerned with being permanently in our hearts than being permanently inked on our skin. *Go figure.*

WHO IS JESUS REALLY

We love the idea of Jesus, but not the *actual* Jesus. We have our own imaginary version that fits our beliefs. It may even contradict Jesus. When He was on the earth, people were confused about who He *really* was. Some said and still say today that Jesus was a good man, while others say He was a prophet.

"'But what about you?'" he asked. "Who do you say I am?'" Simon Peter answered, "You are the Messiah, the Son of the living God.'" Matthew 16:15-16

When Jesus began to predict His own death and resurrection, Peter didn't understand. After all, Jesus was the Messiah! He rebuked Jesus, saying "Never, Lord! This shall never happen to you!" (Matthew 16:22). You see, the disciples were under the impression that the Messiah was sent to overthrow the Romans and restore Israel to its former glory. If we have accepted that Jesus is the Son of God, then we must understand that His main objective isn't to help us prosper on Earth.

Jesus instructed a healed leper to be silent – he was to go to the temple and offer a sacrifice. His obedience was supposed to be the testimony, *not his healing.* But he couldn't help himself; he spread the news of the miracle in lieu of being obedient. Because of this, Jesus was not able to enter the town (Mark 1:45).

Jesus doesn't want us blurting out that He is Lord while simultaneously disobeying Him any more than PETA (People For Ethical Treatment of Animals) would want a *prize-winning cockfighter* as their spokesman. Our testimony is nothing without action. As living sacrifices, our lives are the real testimony. Indiscriminately spewing Jesus's name only makes it harder for Him to enter our homes, workplaces, and communities. We limit Him; we make it difficult for people to find out who Jesus is *really.*

BATTLE RAP

"At that time the disciples came to Jesus and asked, 'Who, then, is the greatest in the kingdom of heaven?'" Matthew 18:1

Mainstream hip-hop music is mostly about glorifying oneself. The epitome of this self-glorification materializes in the form of a rap battle. Two individuals duke it out, freestylin' from the top of the dome. A crowd encircles them, carefully listening to every line. They ultimately hail the rapper with most clever insults as the greater.

The disciples once argued about who was going to be the greatest. Even the mother of James and John asked that her sons sit on the right and left of Jesus in His kingdom. "Jesus called the twelve, and said, 'Anyone who wants to be first must be the very last, and the servant of all'" (Mark 9:35).

We work so hard to make ourselves look greater than others. But instead of exalting ourselves to *be* served, Jesus teaches that our service is what exalts us. When we try to be greater or holier than our brothers and sisters, it shows that we're still confused about Jesus's purpose.

YOU GOT SERVED!

"... just as the Son of Man did not come to be served, but to serve, and to give his life as a ransom for many." Matthew 20:28

When Jesus washed the feet of the disciples, He was exemplifying humility and servitude. Peter was confused and upset, initially refusing Jesus. Washing feet was a slave's job, and he couldn't grasp why his master would stoop so low. "Jesus answered, 'Unless I wash you, you have no part with me.' 'Then, Lord,' Simon Peter replied, 'not just my feet but my hands and head as well!'" (John 13:8-9)

God isn't some boss who's commanding us to obey or go to hell – He knows we're weak. He knows we're self-serving. He exemplified leadership, not with pride but with humility. He became flesh, was born in a stable, grew up in Nazareth (a.k.a. the ghetto), and He served people. On Palm Sunday, the Almighty rode in on a donkey instead of a stallion. And when the people turned on Him, He stayed humble, even unto death. *He is the greatest.*

 Be the most humble person you know – putting the humility of others to shame! Your humility speaks volumes, so make sure it says, "You call that humility?"

Even when we try to be humble, we hope everyone notices it. For example, if I were to scrub my church's toilets, vacuums the floor, or take out the trash, I would hope that someone notices my work – so they will think highly of me. "Gee, that guy is selfless." But true humility doesn't seek to be noticed.

"Be careful not to practice your righteousness in front of others to be seen by them. If you do, you will have no reward from your Father in heaven. So when you give to the needy, do not announce it with trumpets, as the hypocrites do in the synagogues and on the streets, to be honored by others." Matthew 6:1-2

Jesus didn't come to fit our definition of greatness. He came with His own standard – one that flips ours on its head. When we think of greatness – of a God who is worthy to be praised – we want Him to come in the form of what we already praise. We're prone to expect God to enter this world in a palace, not a stable. We think of a God who is strikingly handsome, *not average or ugly*; a God of might, *not a God of humility*. We want Him to validate our existing ideology – to fit our representation of greatness.

So you want to be great?

"You don't know what you are asking,' Jesus said to them. 'Can you drink the cup I am going to drink?'" Matthew 20:22

Many of the early disciples were put to death for their faith. They drank from His cup, and shared in His suffering. Upon Peter's own crucifixion, he told them to hang him upside down, for he was not worthy to die like his Master. Like Christ, he exhibited humility even in death. But neither humility nor death is a part of Jesus that we want. We don't want all of Him; just a piece of Him – *a Jesus piece.*

THE FIRST STONE

I've always taken pride in my ability to accept positive criticism – unlike negative people who just fire back. For instance, a close friend once questioned a slightly judgmental comment I made via Twitter, so I did the right thing – *I fired back!*

I had expressed my displeasure with a Gospel music video that was produced by the most unlikely of artists, *Destiny's Child*. Unlike most Christian-contemporary songs that are filled with double entendre – the lyrics capable of being directed towards God or girlfriend – Beyoncé and company, were specifically using Jesus's name! *Blasphemy!*

I remembered that R. Kelly – another producer of sexually-charged music – had released a Gospel album suspiciously around the time that he was facing allegations of sexual misconduct. It was beyond obvious to me that these praise songs were not only disingenuous, but that angelic forces were ferociously swatting them down before they could reach God.

Cover your ears, Lord!

I considered the contradiction to be clear, but my friend disagreed. "I think you're wrong," he calmly explained. He's often given me sound advice, so I gave him the benefit of the doubt, responding, "What?! Are you insane?!"

This time he was wrong. Anyone can see that Beyoncé should not be praising God! Well... not while simultaneously releasing lustful music videos. Repent first, Bey, then we can talk Jesus.

He agitated me a bit further, gently reminding me of my sketchy record. He then added that my persona didn't stop me from writing a book on Christianity. *Enough!* Now I was enraged! This wasn't apples to apples. This wasn't positive criticism. *This was an all out character assassination!!*

"What makes you, or me [he tactfully adds], any better than them?" he retorted.

I didn't say I was better; *I only implied it.*

Our texting debate raged on. Well, I raged; he was relatively calm. Obviously, when compared to a secular musician, I, a Christian, had the moral high-ground. *Duhhh.* I argued that it was ridiculous that the same artist is singing about both sex and Jesus – conveniently leaving out that my iTunes playlist contained songs about both sex and Jesus. Still, this was not the same. These musicians are public figures who commit sins on a *grand scale!*

I rest my case. Confident in how I formulated my argument and closing statement, I awaited his inevitable concession. Three dots appeared on the screen, alerting me that he was typing – *probably a sincere apology.*

"Does scale matter to God?" he replied.

My argument collapsed. It was entirely based on a scale. I had determined that the musicians were worse sinners than I. I was *less* of a hypocrite. We've all sinned and fallen short of Jesus's standard, yet the premise of my case was that I sinned *less*, that my sin was not as bad, not as public.

I had put my focus on the wrong thing. I wasn't called to judge; I was called to love. Sure, the musicians may have been broadcasting conflicted interests, but I shouldn't see that as an opportunity to pounce – that's where I went wrong. If I was truly concerned about correcting a believer's contradiction, I would do it with love. I would do it in confidence, *not on Twitter.*

WE'RE BAAA-AAACK!

"Jesus straightened up and asked her, 'Woman, where are they? Has no one condemned you?' 'No one, sir,' she said. 'Then neither do I condemn you,' Jesus declared. 'Go now and leave your life of sin.'"
John 8:10-11

The religious leaders had brought a prostitute who was 'caught in the act' before Jesus, to trap Him. Instead, He wrote in the sand. Some speculate that He revealed their hidden sins; we don't know.

There were three flaws in their reasoning:
First, they assumed that the prostitute's sin was worse that theirs.
Second, they left out the man with whom she was caught. This itself was breaking the same law with which they sought to judge her. *Their interest was selective punishment.*
Third, and most importantly, they wanted Jesus specifically to condemn her.

"Where are your accusers?" Jesus asked.

We're right here! In fact, we have represented you, Jesus. We're making the same flaws: assuming that our sin is less, selectively judging, and worst of all, we've used you, specifically, to condemn others.

Sure, we don't say we're better; we just imply it.

It's so easy to judge, because all it takes is to think that you're better than someone. Surely, you consider yourself better than *someone*, right? Perhaps it's someone who's on drugs, someone who's overweight, someone who's gay, someone who's on welfare, someone who's ungrateful, someone who's promiscuous, or someone who's *judgmental.*

"When a man is getting better he understands more and more clearly the evil that is still left in him. When a man is getting worse he understands his own badness less and less." -C.S. Lewis

Being judgmental is very unpopular, which is interesting because we all are – to some degree. I've found that I judge people all day long. I never noticed it until I tried not to judge. I judge people by race, religion, behavior – whatever. I judge people who judge me. Sometimes I feel like I'm surrounded by inconsiderate idiots – people with zero etiquette. All day long, all I see is people's faults, and never my own.

WHO DIED AND MADE YOU JUDGE?

The more people I judge, the more I realize I need to be forgiven for assuming Christ's role as judge. He didn't die and make me judge, He died to direct us to mercy. As a Christian, I can't even judge the judgmental. I can only check myself – an action that leads me to drop the stone I didn't realize I was gripping.

I can only bring awareness, bring light. It begins with the realization that I've fallen short of Christ's standard. Let Jesus be the judge. In His eyes, it doesn't matter who sins more or less. In fact, the ones who think they have the moral high-ground are at high-risk.

SURROUNDED BY SAVAGES

Our burden for those we view as lost is reminiscent of Rudyard Kipling's heart-warming 19th century poem, *The White Man's Burden*. It was a burden that beseeched civilized men to tame and rule the savages. Sure, they would resist, but ultimately, their descendants would be the benefactors of enslavement, colonization, and genocide.

It's the cliché, yet romantic story about good versus evil; light versus dark... *skin*.

I admit, there were some atrocities committed in spreading the Gospel. *But please be reasonable.* To prevent recipients from 'shooting the messenger,' the messengers had to come shooting.

When an individual lives to a certain standard, sometimes, all he/she can see is people who aren't living up to that same standard. The individual senses a 'burden' to correct others, for their own good! – even if others don't recognize his/her standard. At face value, the individual fancies himself better than those savages.

For example, let's say you hold yourself to a standard of hygiene – one you assume is reasonable. You shower, brush your teeth, and change your underwear every day. You would instantly be revolted by someone who does not.

I visited my family in Africa when I was 10 years old. The first thing I noticed was that everyone smelled bad. The second thing I noticed is that *no one noticed.* Savages!

Is this not how we see non-believers and hypocrites, as savages? Godless people who indulge in sexual desire, ambition, greed, envy – all the vices we're acting like we've tamed. Our burden isn't to bring them to the light, but to show that we're *less savage.*

Our obedience to God becomes something we take pride in, instead of something we were only able to do by grace (Romans 11:5). It can happen to anyone who manages to string together some consistency in doing good deeds or obeying the *Ten Commandments.* We think God must be pleased that we have been paying tithes, abstaining from pre-marital sex, or abstaining from *as much* pre-marital sex. Without realizing it, our faith becomes based on earning God's mercy and compassion. And all we can see is others who are not earning it. *Savages!*

COMPARE AND CONDEMN

"They theoretically admit themselves to be nothing in the presence of this phantom God, but are really all the time imagining how He approves of them and thinks them far better than ordinary people: that is, they pay a pennyworth of imaginary humility to Him and get out of it a pound's worth of pride towards their fellow-men." -C.S. Lewis

In *Mere Christianity*, C.S. Lewis elaborates on the way in which pride smuggles itself into the very core of our faith. It creeps in when our walk with Jesus makes us feel good, or rather, *better* than someone else – which is all it takes to judge someone else.

No one takes pride in being good, smart, or attractive; we take pride in being better, smarter, or more attractive.

Lewis explains that all the vices – greed, lust, anger, drunkenness, etc. –are only flea bites in comparison to pride. In fact, those vices can be eradicated *with* pride itself, as we consider them to be beneath us. Satan "is perfectly content to see you becoming chaste and brave and self-controlled provided, all the time, he is setting up in you the Dictatorship of Pride."

Many of us Christians have traded in a smaller sin for a bigger, more dangerous one – it somehow slips under the radar. It not only prevents us from being a part of Christ's kingdom, but it blocks others as well. *It compares and condemns.*

This is the reason why it's so important to examine if our faith is genuine. Christ was humble, and to be His followers, we must be humble. The first step towards humility is the realization that we are proud. And if we think of pride as someone else's struggle, that we ourselves are not judgmental, we are all the more full of it.

"Search me, God, and know my heart; test me and know my anxious thoughts. See if there is any offensive way in me, and lead me in the way everlasting." Psalms 139:23-24

THE LAST STONE

Like many progressive Christians, I have been evolving on my view of homosexuals. I've slowly conceded to the *radical* approach, 'hate the sin, not the sinner.' *I'm still struggling to register it.* Ok, gay sinner, you can come to church now. (Although, you may be subject to overwhelming gossip and scrutiny.)

We don't discriminate, well, *publicly.*

Let's be honest: we judge gays. We love to point out that the Bible (a book many of them don't regard) *clearly* says that they will not enter the kingdom of heaven. *Done.* Case closed! Some think, "You're gay? You're going to hell! I'm no bigot, but I bet there may even be a special hell for you."

But before we revise *Dante's Inferno,* a 14ᵗʰ century story about the stages of hell, to place homosexuals as the bunk-mates of Brutus and Judas, let's consider this: We may be going to hell ourselves.

"Jesus said to them, 'Truly I say to you that the tax collectors and prostitutes will get into the kingdom of God before you.'" Matthew 21:31

Picture Jesus telling self-righteous, outwardly devout people that those whom they perceive of as scum will enter the kingdom of God before they do. *Infuriating!*

Do homosexuals sin? According to our faith, yes. But our attitudes towards them (according to our faith), is a greater sin! Instead of using God's word as a light, we use it as a tool to judge. Failing to see that when we judge others, we judge ourselves (Romans 2:1-3).

We like to pick and choose what sins to condemn. We fight to protect the sanctity of marriage from lesbians and gays, but not so much from divorce. We fight abortion, but neglect the dying. We fight violence in the media... wait, who are we kidding? We don't fight that.

TOLERATING TOLERANCE

As our society becomes increasingly tolerant of the LGBT community, we either: 1) fight them tooth and nail – stopping short of picketing 'God hates fags,' or 2) shrug our shoulders and somewhat accept them, with the contingency that they immediately change their sinfulness.

Did we immediately change *our* sinfulness?

Imagine if the church had been first to embrace and love homosexuals, you know, before Hollywood did? *Wait, let's take it back a few decades.* Imagine if the church had been first to embrace and love blacks, you know, before the Civil Rights Movement?

What a missed opportunity to touch people who were marginalized by society. Instead, the church marginalized them as well – even segregated the seating in the sanctuary! *Perhaps they hoped heaven would also be segregated.*

My parents immigrated to America to escape Ethiopian communism in the early 1980's. They were shocked by racial discrimination, especially when it was demonstrated by those in the church. My father not-so-fondly recollects being called a 'nigger' at work, and being treated like a 'nigger' at church. Even the pastor refused to shake his hand.

To make things worse, the assistant dean of the missionary university he attended tried to force them back to Africa when he found out that my mother was pregnant. Apparently he had foiled their master plan to become American citizens!

They escaped religious persecution in Ethiopia only to be persecuted by the religious in America. The church should have been the place to find shelter, the light in the darkness; instead, it was even darker.

Is this Christianity? Many bemoan the moral decay of our society – once a 'Christian nation.' Some say we need to return to our roots! Hopefully their revival doesn't include the reinstatement of slavery, Jim Crow Laws, or the genocide of any remaining Native Americans. Some Christians cry, "They took prayer out of public schools!" But sadly, the type of prayer that was in schools was the type that did not permit people of all races to participate.

How can our nation be Christian if our churches aren't even Christian?

I once found it appalling to compare the discrimination against homosexuals to that of African Americans. Not only were blacks subject to slavery, lynching, and segregation, but they were born black and gays were... uhhh. It seems that there's some debate. Some say they were born gay; others have clearly changed their preference. *But that has nothing to do with our responsibility to exhibit Christ's love to all.*

We may not be picketing against them, but we may still see them as our enemies. Even if they come to church, *it's clear,* they're not like us.

There was a time not too long ago when the overwhelming majority of American society had nothing but contempt for the LGBT community – a time when hatred for gays was shared across the board, from the deeply religious to misogynistic rappers. Of course, Christians didn't agree with rap culture's sexually-charged, profanity-laced, and violence-glorifying lyrics, but we were united by our hate for homosexuals!

But now, the world around us is 'dropping the stone.' Slowly but surely, society is renouncing its bigotry against homosexuals, just as it had done with blacks. Not because of Christians, *but despite Christians.* We, the representation of Christ, are now holding the last stone.

Not only did Jesus command us not to judge, but He also called us to show His love to those who are being judged. Consider this: when the Pharisees brought the prostitute before Jesus, asking whether they should stone her, *they wanted to kill her.* Her world was against her. But God's love rescued and changed her life.

Some may see the key word as 'change.' Others either find offense to 'change,' or insist that they can't. So let's continue the dispute.

DISPUTING THE DISPUTE

"For every complex problem there is an answer that is clear, simple, and wrong." - H.L. Mencken

I'm not offering a solution to the 'homosexuals in church' conversation any more than I could have offered the rescued prostitute a new way to make a living. After all, I am neither a redeemed homosexual, nor a redeemed prostitute – not to imply the two are similar, *as some would be delighted by the notion.*

The liberal, progressive side would question why there's anything to resolve. To them, the problem is the fact that there's a problem. "Gays were born this way!" What kind of God sends someone to hell for being born a certain way? *Oh yes!* The same God that sends an *indigenous Amazonian tribe* who have never heard the name 'Jesus' *to hell!"*

They either reject Christianity or reconcile the issue with a compromised interpretation.

To the conservative, traditional side, it's a clear and cut-throat, 'gays will not be saved' approach – until a family member comes out as gay. Moderate Christians have come to this realization and don't want to pick between the two sides.

There are two main arguments, "I did not choose to be this way," and "Yes you did, you wicked sodomite!" There are some new moderate arguments, which turn out to be repackaged originals – anecdotal examples of people who did or did not re-hab from gay therapy. Either solution seems asinine to the other.

"The problem isn't the problem. The problem is your attitude about the problem."- Captain Jack Sparrow

My dispute is with the dispute itself: has the church missed yet another opportunity to reach the rejected? Or do we even care? The church should be a place where one finds shelter; not a place one *escapes from* to find shelter. Many of us don't hate homosexuality because it's a sin; we hate it because it's *homosexuality!*

If we hated sin that much, we would hate the sin within ourselves – our attitude about the problem. The correlation between Westernized Christian hatred for blacks and hatred for homosexuals is this: we've masked *bigotry* with *hate of sin*. Christianity's adherents have once again weaponized the Gospel.

Of course, gays can't recall a specific moment when they chose to be gay. When did we *choose* to be self-righteous? Did we choose to be unforgiving, prideful, or judgmental? Did we choose to be a terrible representation of Christ, *or were we always this way?*

The real difference between us is this: *straight believers* know specifically what *gay believers* didn't choose to be. It's hidden sin versus visible sin – both of which we may never reconcile. Obviously, one who believes in the Bible shouldn't expect to re-write it and still consider it sacred. *That would be foolish.* So would trying to make someone, who didn't consider it sacred, abide by it.

ONLY THE WEAK SURVIVE

Paul boasted in his weakness. It's weakness that relates. It's weakness that reaches. It's weakness that makes Jesus strong. This issue is one that must be championed by those who are (and I regret having to use this word) ex-gay. If one can successfully, happily, and with free will overcome same-sex orientation, we must be supportive. They're in a tough position. Conservatives hate them for being gay, and liberals hate them for being ex-gay.

Some, who are choosing to stay celibate, are on the receiving end of severe scrutiny – liberals consider them to be self-hating and brainwashed. However, it seems the only thing the celibate ex-gays hate, *is being called self-hating and brainwashed.* Aren't progressives the ones who originally advocated for them, on the basis of their right to choose? It seems like the tolerant have become intolerant.

(Note: The reason I regret having to use the word 'ex-gay' is because we wouldn't naturally use 'ex' in reference to ourselves. For example: ex-fornicator, ex-idolator, or ex-liar.)

I am not advocating that gay believers become celibate, nor get married to someone they are not attracted to. I am advocating that we love them, whether or not they choose to reconcile the clear conflict of interest. Straight believers don't understand what it's like to be forced to pick between orientation and faith, especially when society is now telling us it's natural. The one thing we must avoid is seeking a church where the clergy will tell us whatever we want to hear.

"For the time will come when people will not put up with sound doctrine. Instead, to suit their own desires, they will gather around them a great number of teachers to say what their itching ears want to hear." 2 Timothy 4:3

A CHRISTIAN SOCIETY

The fight isn't whether or not Christianity can approve of homosexuality –this can only be done by rewriting, or grossly misinterpreting the Bible (*which some denominations have no problem doing*). Rather, the fight against gay marriage is in regards to change in social morality. We Christians are desperately trying to salvage the resemblance between social morality and Christian morality. But why? Social morality doesn't save souls; *it only controls the masses.*

Do we want Christianity to be known for controlling the masses? Well, it's too late for that.

"They worship me in vain; their teachings are merely human rules. You have let go of the commands of God and are holding on to human traditions." Mark 7:7-8

As social morality, or – as we Christians like to call it – moral decay progresses (or regresses), the church finds itself in a politically polarizing position. Why continue wasting our efforts to instill Christian morals in society? Why try to fix an external issue that has an internal cause? As a church, we must exemplify true worship, not tradition. Perhaps then, the lost will praise God with us and not curse Him because of us.

To reach the lost, to reach our own, we must speak their language. Paul became all things to all people. We too can only effectively carry out our mission by relating – which doesn't mean we interpret the Bible differently to accommodate human weakness. It means we shouldn't act like we don't have any weaknesses ourselves.

Our approach to rapidly changing social norms shouldn't be a relaxed attitude to sin, nor a focus on restoring our values. It should be to look inward: an examination of ourselves.

Would I like to raise children in a society that doesn't glorify lust, greed, and pride? Yes, absolutely. Am I afraid that my Christian views are becoming increasingly marginalized? Yes, absolutely. Is our country turning into a Godless society? *No, it already was.* It only had the superficial appearance of a God-fearing society – which is exactly what we're fighting for, *superficiality.*

"You clean the outside of the cup and dish, but inside they are full of greed and self-indulgence. Blind Pharisee! First clean the inside of the cup and dish, and then the outside also will be clean." Matthew 23:25-26

In *Mere Christianity*, C.S. Lewis admits, "Christian society would be what we now call Leftist." He engages us on how we have cherry picked what parts of the Bible we, as a society, want to follow. We can think of a few things we've selectively allowed in our 'Christian society': corporate greed, fiscal irresponsibility, divorce, discrimination, social injustice.

Lewis, however, brings up something we've not only turned a blind eye to, but we've built our entire economic system on – *usury.* One of the greatest sins in the Bible is lending at interest. Behold, our nation is drowning in debt to Visa, Master-Card, and China. Student loans have reached a trillion dollars! Some are trapped getting a cash advance to pay off a cash advance. We, the Christian society, have ignored this and are now wondering why the rich get richer and the middle class is being wiped out.

But now that homosexuals are redefining social morality, *we're up in arms!* This is where we have drawn the line: *not* at becoming a country that imprisons hoards people, in both jail and debt, *not* the corporate and pharmaceutical control of our government, *not* social inequality. *Homosexuality!* And we won't be cherry picking this time.

Or will we?

This excerpt from *Mere Christianity* reflects my exact conclusion to this section:

"And now, before I end, I am going to venture on a guess as to how this section has affected any who have read it. My guess is that there are some Leftist people among them who are very angry that it has not gone further in that direction, and some people of an opposite sort who are angry because they think it has gone much too far. If so, that brings us right up against the real snag in all this drawing up of blueprints for a Christian society. Most of us are not really approaching the subject in order to find out what Christianity says: we are approaching it in the hope of finding support from Christianity for the views of our own party...

A Christian society is not going to arrive until most of us really want it: and we are not going to want it until we become fully Christian. I may repeat "Do as you would be done by" till I am black in the face, but I cannot really carry it out till I love my neighbour as myself: and I cannot learn to love my neighbour as myself till I learn to love God: and I cannot learn to love God except by learning to obey Him."

PART 3:
WHAT'S LOVE GOT TO DO WITH IT?

LOVE: *Thy neighbor*

A 'one-two' punch symbolizes getting hit twice, the second blow coming before we can recover from the first. When the Pharisees tried to trap Jesus with a theological question regarding what the greatest commandment was, He hit 'em with the ol' one-two. "Love God, pow! Love your neighbor, pow *pow!*" *Slightly paraphrased.* Basically, all of God's laws hinge on these two commandments (Matthew 22:40).

THE GATED COMMUNITY

"But he wanted to justify himself, so he asked Jesus, 'And who is my neighbor?'" Luke 10:29

There's a sense of security within a gated community. We may not know everyone in it, but we know that everyone is of the same socio-economic status. We felt even safer before the indiscriminate passage of the 'Fair Housing Act.' Intuitively, we've been able counter this intrusion with community watch programs and racial profiling.

We're only comfortable granting access to people who share our values, appearances, and traditions. And we long to gate our community in heaven as it is on earth.

My church went to minister to people on Skid Row–the roughest part of downtown Los Angeles. This area is populated by the homeless, criminals, and prostitutes. These people have hit rock bottom, figuratively and perhaps literally. *Surely they would be receptive to Jesus!*

As we walked around a park, handing out flyers and inviting them to church (not ours of course, rather the local 'urban-rehabilitation-church', which would be more fitting for them), we quickly realized how difficult it was. They were used to people like us, and they weren't interested. We began to retreat to each other; *ministering was a bad idea!*

 Post your good deed on social media *and get the heck out of there!* After all, you'll get the same amount of likes whether you were there for 3 hours or 3 minutes.

Inwardly, we bemoaned leaving our comfort zones. It was Saturday morning! We should be in bed eating cereal and watching television. Instead, we were out getting rejected by society's rejected.

It wasn't until we did the unthinkable – we joined them – that they began to accept us. For a moment, they saw us as more than people who were trying to spread a religion. *Which was exactly what we were trying to do.*

As we played dominoes and basketball with them, it clicked! Jesus didn't roll up to tax collectors, prostitutes, and sinners with flyers like, "Yo, come to synagogue this Sabbath. Well, not *my* synagogue, but the one specialized to rehabilitate you lowlives." Rather, He sat with them, ate with them. He ministered to them on their level, with love.

I thought, "How much of an impact would I have on *these* people if I came back next Saturday on my own – without the church flyers? What if they saw how much I really cared!?"

I never returned.

"So when Peter went up to Jerusalem, the circumcised believers criticized him and said, 'You went into the house of uncircumcised men and ate with them.'" Acts 11:2-3

Fellow Christians frowned on Peter because he visited the home of Cornelius the Centurion, a.k.a. *Uncircumcised Gentile*. But now that most of us Christians are Gentiles, we've found other people to frown on. When Jesus was asked who 'my neighbor' was, He responded with a parable.

Here we go again. In this one, a filthy, disgusting, half-breed Samaritan is the hero! The Jews hated the Samaritans because they were a mixed race and they worshipped God at a different location.

We've all heard the story. Some poor guy was beat up and robbed on the road. A priest and a Levite passed the wounded and dying man, but a Samaritan saved him. *Great story, Jesus; you've pissed off everyone.* Telling this parable to Jews was like telling Klansmen that a mulatto rescued a beaten white man! *Neighbor, please!*

MAXIMUM SECURITY COMMUNITY

In the last chapter, I touched on the racist treatment my parents encountered attending conservative American churches. I had quite a different church experience. I was raised in a church comprised of Ethiopian immigrants.

For me, growing up in church was much more than religion or a sense of community; *it was a sense of culture.* My closest friends were Ethiopian Christians. We shared a bond that transcended faith. Church was a place where we, Ethiopians, could fellowship with other Ethiopians. It was a place for us to eat traditional food, wear traditional clothes, and sing traditional songs – all of which, as a kid, I hated. But ultimately, church was a place where our culture and our faith intersected.

More or less, what kept me going to church was the culture, *not the faith.* I could identify with everyone there. And the love we had for each other – which was based on our commonality – was strong. We were incredibly close knit.

As a young adult, I noticed that we were beginning to have, for the first time, some African American guests. And by guests, I mean regular attendees. *It felt odd.* This is *our church,* what are *they* doing here? Who is responsible for bringing these non-Ethiopians to the house of the Lord!?

I felt a little threatened. "These guys can't fool me," I thought to myself, "they're only here to look for girls!" So I did my best to make them feel uncomfortable and unwelcome.

Terrible, I know. The more I allow the Spirit to search my heart, the more darkness He reveals.

"Nobody is more dangerous than he who imagines himself pure in heart; for his purity, by definition, is unassailable." -James A. Baldwin

I debated my fellow Ethiopian Christians who didn't feel as threatened. "Don't be naïve; we know what they're here for!" Some even attended the traditional service and asked for a translator. I thought, did they have trouble finding an English-speaking church? Surely they wouldn't need to bother anyone for an interpreter at 'Crenshaw Chapel.'

I was convinced that church was not just a place of faith, but of culture and community. "Would it not be odd if I attended a Korean church and asked them for a translator?" I argued. "Would they not be within their right to suspect me? Why not find a church with your type of people?"

I neglected to divulge that I myself had attended black churches to do the exact thing that I suspected these guys of doing – look for girls. "But this was not the same," I rationed to myself. "We were the minority." There were only a handful of us Ethiopians. *I had to protect my community.*

The same basis on which I demonized conservative American churches for racially mistreating my family, I mistreated others. Jesus said that if we could truly see, our guilt would remain (John 9:41). *I was guilty of the same exact sin.* I wanted to keep the church gated because it wasn't about communion with Christ, but communion with people like me.

"If you love those who love you, what reward will you get? Are not even the tax collectors doing that? And if you greet only your own people, what are you doing more than others? Do not even pagans do that?" Matthew 5:46-47

KEEP YOUR FRIENDS CLOSE, YOUR ENEMIES CLOSER

It's easy to love people who love us, but how can we love an enemy? Can we love someone – scratch that – love *everyone* despite conflicting views and beliefs? We may need to reassess whether this whole Christianity thing is for us. It's not easy to respond to hate with love. When someone flips us off, cuts in front of us in traffic, or talks bad about us behind our backs, we naturally retaliate.

Anger and hatred expose a lack of inner peace, *Jesus's peace.* It's supposed to surpass all understanding (Philippians 4:7). But if we're not rooted in Christ, we instinctively bite back. A brief moment of anger can void our entire testimony. If we would only see every interaction as a form of witnessing, we may reconsider how we react to negative situations.

"Then Agrippa said to Paul, 'Do you think that in such a short time you can persuade me to be a Christian?'" Acts 26:28

The Apostle Paul truly loved his enemies, even as they imprisoned and falsely accused him. He used every opportunity to share the love of Christ. If we had a piece of that same love, it would shape our actions towards others. We would recognize that, although we may not be able to swiftly persuade someone to be a Christian, we may swiftly persuade someone not to be.

YOU CALL YOURSELF A CHRISTIAN?!

I tried to reason with him, but he refused to comply. I felt cheated. So I went for the jugular. I attacked the very essence of who he was, yelling, "You call yourself a Christian?!"

Let's go back three years. I had found a reasonably priced vacancy three blocks from the beach. In my interview with the apartment manager – which was all about assessing whether I would be a good tenant – I casually mentioned that I was a Christian. Well what-do-ya-know, so was he!

I figured he was. He was slightly goofy – had this 'Ned Flanders' thing about him. Am I generalizing? *Yes.* I figured I was at a disadvantage since I was a young black guy, so I leveraged my 'Christian card.' "It'd be a wonderful card to pull," I thought, unless he turns out to be an atheist.

 **Tip** Use the 'Christian card' as leverage when you would otherwise have none. You need customers? Call your business a 'Christian business'. You need someone to buy your crappy music? Call it 'Christian rap'. You need an 'A' in philosophy? *Keep this card in your pocket.*

I began sharing pleasantries with my new-found 'brother-in-Christ'. *This was too easy.* Surely, he would pick me over any non-believer candidates.

Three years later, I moved out. By then, I had soured of him, and I suspect he had soured of me. I had bent a few rules. Smoking wasn't allowed, but that doesn't include hookah and medical herb, *right?* We still managed to remain cordial. I was a nice guy all the way up until he returned only a fraction of my deposit. I felt *very* cheated.

I tried to reason with him. I wished I was able to employ the 'brother-in-Christ' card, but cut the crap: I had lived there for three years. He knew me. He refused to comply, so I took off my nice-guy persona. He was now my 'enemy-in-Christ.'

Our cordial masks were gone; our gloves were off! We hurled insults and curse words – well, I did. He raged too, in his Ned Flanders-type of way. I thought, "How could this man, who was currently attending seminary, cheat me?!" So I went for the jugular, I attacked the very essence of who he was, yelling, "You call yourself a Christian?!"

Click. He hung up.

It felt so good saying it. It was the dagger, a deathblow! (*to our conversation, at least*). We began our relationship – manager/tenant – on the grounds of Christian faith, and ended it on the grounds of Christian faith.

Alpha and Omega!

How could a Christian cheat me? Surely he was not a true Christian. The irony of the situation being that, he could have said the same of me. To him, I was an impostor. To me, he was an impostor. How do you say, "you need Jesus," to someone who claims to have Him?

Not only did I lack love for my neighbor, literally, I lacked love for my Christian neighbor. I put on a facade until I didn't need to anymore. In that moment, it felt clear to me that he was not a Christian and clear to him that I was not either.

NOTHING MATTERS BUT LOVE

"If I have the gift of prophecy and can fathom all the mysteries and all knowledge, and if I have faith that can move mountains, but do not have love, I am nothing." 1 Corinthians 13:2

A Nobel Peace Prize may be awarded to one who fathoms mysteries, has great knowledge, or does social good. This is the world's highest honor, but without love, it means nothing. Christ did all of those things, but the greatest thing He did, was love. Without love, our world would be an intelligent design without a path to its designer. Crucifix? Ha! Why would Jesus allow Himself to be sacrificed to reconcile the gap between God and mere mortals? *Love.* And if we're truly His disciples, the realization of His love for us must reciprocate into love for others.

MARKET VALUES

"If you show special attention to the man wearing fine clothes and say, 'Here's a good seat for you,' but say to the poor man, 'You stand there' or 'Sit on the floor by my feet,' have you not discriminated among yourselves and become judges with evil thoughts?" James 2:3-4

We're familiar with statements like, "He's worth 100 million dollars." There has always been a concept that someone's life can mean more than another's. After all, you can't equate the value of a C.E.O. to that of a street hustler. Today, we call it a person's net worth. It's the accumulation of a person's assets and cash, minus their liabilities.

We love people who have great net worth. Many times, their fortunes are directly linked to celebrity status. We think it's so awesome when a celebrity becomes a Christian; maybe we can chat with them in heaven! If they come to our church, we'll seat them in the front and even announce their presence. We shower them with love.

God is not a respecter of persons, but we are. *Why?* Because we love wealth, status, and celebrity. So naturally, we gravitate to those who have attained it. We ignore impoverished areas of the world, places where people are selling themselves or their children into virtual slavery. But what choice do they have? Or a better question is, what worth do they have?

Tip The needy are out of sight, out of mind... until that World Vision commercial comes on. Well, God gave you DVR for a reason! *Fast-Forward.*

During the African Holocaust, blacks were not considered people, but rather, property. Their values were commensurate to their ability to serve their masters. Today, slavery is an international injustice; freedom is unanimously perceived of as a human right. Nevertheless, the way we appraise the value of the people remains the same. Their worth is commensurate to how well they serve us; not how God served them.

1ST WORLD PROBLEMS

If you're from America, a nation known for power and wealth, then you may have realized that we're hated around the world. *Or maybe you haven't.* 'MERICA!! Should we be demonized because we're born richer?

Does our privilege make us indifferent? So much so that it's difficult to relate? The Apostle Paul said, "I have become all things to all people so that by all possible means I might save some" (1 Corinthians 9:22). To the educated, he was a scholarly orator, to the layman he was a tentmaker. Whether witnessing to Jew or Gentile, he never allowed indifference to curb his witness.

Americans are hated by the world because of our indifference. When we travel, we expect everyone to speak English and we try to pay in dollars. 'MERICA!! We're culturally insensitive – *we just don't care.* As Comfortable Christians, we've not only disobeyed the second greatest commandment – love your neighbor – we've become indifferent to our neighbor. And the opposite of love isn't hate; *it's indifference.* Loving those who relate to us exhibits our love, but loving those who don't relate exhibits God's love.

LOVE: *Chasin' feelings*

My wife asked a question that I suspect many husbands get asked, "Do you still love me?" The generic response that I suspect many husbands would give is, "Of course, dear." But I didn't want to give her that generic, yet somewhat reassuring reply. *My pause drew some concern.* Either I was not listening, or I was no longer in love with her! I responded, "Babe, it's my responsibility to love you."

She didn't like that one bit. *Responsibility?!* Was I saying that loving her was a chore? Of course not. It's just that, well, we all associate love with the feeling it initially comes with. Then we rely on that feeling to justify our relationships – *the feeling becomes a litmus test.*

The 'love' feeling can get us through hardships; it justifies the effort we put into a commitment. But its purpose and source of strength is dependent on reaching more 'love' feelings. Without realizing it, we begin to rely on the feeling and not the commitment.

"The idea that 'being in love' is the only reason for remaining married really leaves no room for marriage as a contract or promise at all. If love is the whole thing, then the promise can add nothing." -C.S. Lewis

Oftentimes, we're not chasing love; we're chasing a feeling. If it feels right, *it is right.* There's no responsibility, character, or commitment. We do the same with our faith – we base it on how we're feeling. And there's no better feeling to a believer than praise and worship!

FEEL THE SPIRIT

"Yet a time is coming and has now come when the true worshipers will worship the Father in Spirit and in truth, for they are the kind of worshipers the Father seeks." John 4:23

Worship usually takes place during the first half hour of a church service. If we're running late, we usually make up for lost time by worshipping in our car. *It's like spiritual pre-gaming.*

Worship music gets us closer to God, so we think. But there's a chance that we're only emotionally touched by the melody. *Feelings.* We can feel His presence, *right?* Especially when the instruments are in rhythm and the singer's voice is pitch perfect. We're led to lift our hands, close our eyes. We may even shed a tear. *Wow,* that was amazing!

A comment on a YouTube worship video titled *Beautiful Exchange* read, "I love this song, and I'm an atheist!" Perhaps this is a fulfillment of Luke 19, which says, "even the rocks will cry out!" This begs the question, what makes our moment of worship mean any more than that of an atheist? *...or a rock,* for that matter?

EMOTIONAL ROLLER-COASTER

Consider the peculiar way that music sways our emotions – we're moved by the mood of a song. For example, listening to Florida Georgia Line may inspire us to roll our windows down and 'Cruise'. But turning the dial to Eminem's depressing 'Stan' may lead us to 'cruise' right off of a cliff. On the other hand, reggae makes us feel happy – *ev'ryting is irie!*

There's a viral video of a dad who cleverly plays *Buffalo Solider* when his toddler throws a tantrum. Immediately, the child begins bobbing his head and mellows out! Music can induce emotions, but is there any substance to them, or are they just temporary feelings?

Perhaps our worship is just a fleeting high; we're allowing ourselves to get carried away by the mood of the music. Are we even paying attention to the lyrics? Do we even try to fulfill the promises we make to God, or should we be truthful by mumbling disclaimers? Perhaps we could sing, "I Surrender Some," and "Great is My Unfaithfulness."

What actual value does worship music have when compared to a secular song? (Aside from the promotion of our traditional, Christian-Judeo values). Many of us are worship junkies, momentarily caught in the euphoria of worshipping a God who we believe died for us, yet we won't live for Him.

BACKSTAGE PASSES

Picture yourself at a concert of your favorite rap, rock, or pop star. We'll use Jay-Z for this example. You've memorized all the words to his songs as you rap along. *The atmosphere is unreal.* You randomly win backstage passes and a whole week with Jay-Z. As you encounter him after the show, you can barely contain your excitement. You practically worship this guy.

You exchange numbers and he calls in the morning. *Are you really his fan if you aren't available?* Let's say you're busy at work, school, or whatever. "I'll be free in the afternoon," you say. He calls again, but things are still tight. Jay-Z calls again in the evening, but you tell him you're tired from the day. "Maybe tomorrow," you say, as you flip on the television. It's the same story Tuesday, Wednesday, and the whole week.

The atmosphere of worship can feel overwhelming. We can get emotionally caught up as we sing along. But when given the opportunity to remain in 'His presence,' we opt to wait until the next service. When Jesus calls on Monday or Tuesday, we're not available. *Was He ever our God?*

 It may seem ideal to feel God's presence all the time, but what about on Saturday night? Do you really want to feel His presence on the dance floor? Or when you're in bed with your boyfriend/girlfriend? Of course not! So make Sunday your designated 'Feeling God's Presence Day.'

SERVICE WITH A SMILE

"These people honor me with their lips, but their hearts are far from me. They worship me in vain; their teachings are merely human rules." Matthew 15:8-9

God is the only one we worship solely in song. Everything we actually worship comes naturally, without having to sing to it directly. No one looks at their bank account balance, then sings, "How great thou art!" or kneels with reverence before a pornographic website. It's not about what our lips say, but where our hearts are. We're called to have the heart of a servant, *not the lip of a servant.* The insincerity in our worship should appall us; we're giving God lip service.

Lip service*: an avowal of advocacy, adherence, or allegiance expressed in words but not backed by deeds.* (Merriam-Webster)

Few things are more frustrating than getting lip service – especially when you get it all the time. If our worship is only expressed in words and not deeds, we worship in vain. The sermons we hear become mere human rules. What we really worship is what consumes our thoughts, desires, and devotion.

The very first commandment is to have no other gods but God. That's easy because we don't call our gods, 'gods.' But what if we labeled everything we devote our time, thoughts, and resources to as a (fill-in-the-blank) god.

Perhaps we serve a Success god, a Social Media god, or a Boyfriend/Girlfriend god. Whatever it is that we give worth to, we worship. We can't get enough of it and we can't go without it. We need the *feeling* it gives us.

WHAT ARE WE?

"What are we?" This question is often posed in the early stage of a relationship, and depending on the answer, *the final stage*. One person seems to be interested, but won't commit. The reality is, this person still wants the option to date others; perhaps they can do better, or have the other on the side.

In today's secular dating scene, people often have sex before being exclusive – meaning, they're not officially boyfriend/girlfriend. If things continue to go well, then they may ask for exclusivity. But until this point, it's common for the two to have multiple sexual partners. The request to be exclusive can be a dilemma for the person who was asked – especially if he/she only wanted the benefits.

What if Jesus asked, "What are we?" We seem interested during worship, but we can't commit. Are we unsure that Jesus is the best we can do, or do we just prefer to keep Him on the side?

We tell Jesus we love Him on Sunday, but don't call all week. If we do, it's because we want something, perhaps *a late night blessing call.* So, "what are we?" Well, it's complicated – *we only want His benefits.* And part of that is 'feeling the Spirit' in praise and worship.

It's intimacy without commitment.

Just like relationships, true contentment in faith comes when we chase Jesus instead of the feelings initially associated with chasing Jesus. There will be times when we don't feel like praising Him, meditating on His words, and crucifying self-gratification. It's in those moments that our love is tested, and we may break if we're relying on a feeling.

LOVE: *Thy God*

"Love the Lord your God with all your heart and with all your soul and with all your mind and with all your strength." Mark 12:30

The word *love* has lost tremendous value due to our liberal use of it for things we only *like*. (Once again, it's the liberals' fault!) For example, "I love ice cream." We often try to reaffirm meaning for the things we *actually* love by saying, "From the bottom of my heart, *I love ice cream.*" We assume this means that our love is deep, never taking in consideration that there are three more ways to love – with soul, mind, and strength.

MY SOULMATE

By definition, a soulmate is a person who strongly resembles another (Merriam-Webster). They share so many beliefs, attitudes, and attributes that they're practically one person. There are variations, such as soul-brother or soul-sister, which *may or may not* imply a romantic connotation. However, *soulmate* almost always implies love.

The term is often used, or rather, misused in romantic relationships. Some are quick to proclaim a boyfriend/girlfriend a *soulmate* based on surface attributes like taste in music and movies, and not core attributes like character, integrity, and purpose. Often times, the only resemblance shared between the couple is the simultaneous onset of blinding infatuation. But love isn't blind just because the blind call it love.

BREAKING BAD

One cannot simply become the soulmate of another. It's not enough to just do the same things as a couple; you must also have the same desires. For example, let's say a certain woman's passion is to spend every vacation feeding Malaysian children. Her soulmate-boyfriend may go with her because he loves her, even if he'd rather spend every vacation at a resort, perhaps being served by Malaysian children.

She sees no need to compromise because he loves it too! *This is perfect!* Her blissful happiness comes at the cost of his happiness. Surely, at some point he will break character or break up.

We often love Jesus with our hearts, but not our souls. We're just acting when we do stuff He likes – like being patient, kind, and merciful. Inside, we want to be impatient, mean, and judgmental. We try to obey commandments because He desires it, not because we desire it. This type of behavior may eventually lead to breaking character or breaking up.

Speaking of breaking up, in the movie *The Breakup*, Vince Vaughn is perplexed when Jennifer Anniston tells him she wants him to do the dishes *because* he desires to do the dishes – a concept that he, or I, for that matter, *cannot understand.*

If we don't love God with our souls, then any good fruit we've managed to produce – patience, kindness, self-control – are done with self-discipline and practice. And it won't take being a Christian to do them. That's why non-believers may behave better than we do.

No one needs Jesus to be a relatively good person. And if we think that's the purpose of coming to Him, a moral teacher, then we never will come to Him. Even if we struggle with vices that society takes issue with – anger, selfishness, drunkenness – then we'll self-discipline. Following Jesus is not a requirement to be a generally good person; it is, however, a requirement to be born of His Spirit.

FAKE IT TILL YOU MAKE IT!

If we're doing things that are in conflict with Christ's Spirit, but are not in conflict with our spirits, can we honestly say that we love His Spirit with our souls? Does His Spirit testify that we are His children? (Romans 8:16) Do our souls resemble Jesus, or are we only acting like they do?

A popular worship song, *Hosanna*, says, "Break my heart for what breaks yours." King David cried, "Create in me a pure heart, O God" (Psalm 51:10). Essentially, this is a prayer that comes to grips with the fact that we can't 'fake it till we make it.' We need Jesus to transform us to resemble Him – *to be His soulmates.*

King David said, "Oh, how I love your law! I meditate on it all day long" (Psalm 119:97). Keep in mind, this was the same guy who knocked up his soldier's wife and had him killed to conceal it. *I bet he wasn't 'meditating' on it then!* You would assume David would have been disqualified from being a "man after God's own heart" after those types of actions. But loving God doesn't mean we're perfect – it means that we're willing to be corrected. The problem is, we often invite Jesus in, but don't want Him to do work in our dark, selfish hearts.

HEARTS AND MINDS

America! Home of the free! Our troops are like ambassadors of emancipation, bringing democratic deliverance to a captive world! That's why our forces are unanimously welcomed – especially in the Middle East. There we often see images of our flag set ablaze, symbolizing the light and warmth of our military presence.

Well… not exactly.

To us, freedom means having civil liberties, like the *Bill of Rights*. We're fiercely proud of these freedoms – most of which we can't recall. We know the basic ones: freedom of speech, freedom of the press, and (praise the good Lord) the freedom to bear arms! *Bang, bang!*

In countries like Iraq, Afghanistan, and Vietnam, our involvement seemed to only escalate problems. The easy part is bombing out the inhabitants and toppling the government. The hard part is getting them to believe that we know what's best for them.

People from nations we've occupied have mixed, if not negative views towards us, despite our efforts to 'free' them. Perhaps there was a disagreement with our definition of freedom. This disagreement leads to turmoil, rebellion, and instability, hindering the ultimate victory.

"So we must be ready to fight in Vietnam, but the ultimate victory will depend upon the hearts and minds of the people who actually live out there." - Lyndon B. Johnson

Likewise, we Christians keep talking about this freedom we have in Christ. *We want everyone to have it!* Christ came to set the captive free of sin, but c'mon, we'd rather be free *to* sin.

Victory through Christ is contingent on whether we agree with His definition of freedom. We often subscribe to Jesus but don't submit our desire to gratify the flesh. This conflict of interest makes 'having Jesus' kin to a military occupation – leading to inner rebellion, turmoil, and instability.

We often invite Him, thinking His base will serve as an enhancement. But Christ's work is invariably revolutionary, and as a result, laced with discomfort. And the only way His mission will succeed in our lives is if He has our hearts and minds.

NEVER ENOUGH

"Finally, brothers and sisters, whatever is true, whatever is noble, whatever is right, whatever is pure, whatever is lovely, whatever is admirable – if anything is excellent or praiseworthy – think about such things." Philippians 4:8

By meditating on the Word day and night, we can overthrow our greatest adversary: the flesh. That's right: our greatest adversary is not the devil, but ourselves. But in order to do overthrow ourselves, we'd have to delight in Christ's words, perhaps in the way we delight in social media, movies, and music.

As a teenager, I memorized all of Tupac's rap songs. The Internet wasn't big yet, so I couldn't just Google the lyrics. I had to wait for the radio to play the song, record it on tape, then rewind and play it over and over – jotting down every line. *That wasn't it.* Next, I had to read what I wrote as the song played, over and over, to memorize it. In no time, I could recite the rap verbatim – *with the same attitude and ferocity!* I meditated on the lyrics, not out of task, but out of love for my idol.

But could I recite the Beatitudes? Perhaps a few that were hammered into my head, like, "Blessed are the poor in spirit." *Whatever that means.* "Blessed are the meek." *Whatever that means.*

Meditating and memorizing Christ's teaching felt like a task because I didn't love Him like I loved Tupac.

Growing up, my mom frequently asked if I had read my Bible that day. I would read a random verse so I wouldn't have to 'technically' lie. If she asked about the passage, then I would have to technically lie. I found her persistence to be the most irritating on Sundays. "We're on our way to church!" Why the heck would I read my Bible before reading my Bible!?

But if I were on the way to a Tupac concert, would I be upset if the radio started playing his songs? Of course not! *I loved Tupac.*

STRENGTH TRAINING

Tight, long hugs are usually meant to express the strength of one's love for another – or to 'cop a feel'. For example, many women have felt like they were embraced just a bit too long, or a bit too close, by a two-bit opportunist.

We often act like we love Jesus, but we're only trying to 'cop a blessing.' We're merely opportunists if we're seeking to gain divine favor. It's only through testing that we can gauge if one's love has any strength at all. For example, if someone hugged you tight, but wouldn't help you when you're in a bind, the expression of love was only superficial.

The strength of our love for God will be tested, and it won't stand a chance without strict training. It's not something that can be imposed on us by our church or by our parents; *this may actually cause rebellion.* Loving God with our strength is something we train for out of love for Him.

Through my mid-to-late twenties, I was addicted to working out – coming a few bicep curls shy of being a total meathead. Friends would ask to workout with me, but I drove them away with my drill sergeant style. As far as I was concerned, they were giving me a half-baked effort.

For example, my wife joined me once. But she insisted on curling a dumbbell that I figured was way too light. She proved me right when she adjusted her bangs mid-rep! *I was furious.* It was obvious that she was not trying hard enough – she was going at her own pace.

We often go at our own pace in regards to strengthening our faith. Although this yields little result, getting drilled is just as counterproductive.

POINTLESS MEMBERSHIP

There's a popular meme that reads, "Not going to church because of hypocrites is like not going to the gym because of fat people." It's not a bad analogy, but it makes me wonder, how long have the hypocrites stayed as hypocrites, and the fat people as fat people?

Oftentimes, there are two main problems, whether at church or at the gym. The first issue is that our membership may revolve around socializing, and not strict training. We're here to see and be seen.

The second problem is diet. We often bust our butts working out, then fail to properly nourish ourselves. For years, we stay out of shape because the hardest part isn't the exercise; *it's the diet.* Likewise, the hard part isn't obeying commandments; it's consuming daily bread (Matthew 4:4). The hard part is submitting to His Spirit. That's why the Word tells us 'resist the devil and he will flee' *after* 'submit yourself to God'. (James 4:7) We often try to resist on our own strength, which makes giving up our diet of self-gratification seem impossible.

SPOT TRAINING

People often target specific problem areas – a gut, arm fat, or cellulite. But any personal trainer can tell us that there's no such thing as spot training. We can't just do crunches to lose a soft gut. In fact, it may even increase its size by adding muscle under it. *Now,* you have a hard gut. *Now,* you give up.

We have to work on our whole body to resolve problem areas. It takes a proper diet and strict training – *not spot training.* Likewise, focusing on spiritual problem areas, whatever they may be, may result in hardening them. Our spiritual fitness manifests as a whole, as we learn to love God wholly.

DROP THE WEIGHT

I once saw a guy at the gym who had huge muscles and six-pack abs and I thought to myself, *"Man, I'll never be that ripped."* What I was really saying is, "Man, I'll never cut out carbs," or "Man, I'll never be that disciplined."

It reminded me of Jesus's teaching to 'turn the other cheek' (Matthew 5:39). C'mon--*who really does that?* If someone hits me, *on impulse,* I would pummel them! There's no thinking involved, no "Hmmm...what would Jesus do?" *I couldn't imagine being that disciplined.* What I'm really saying is, "Man, I'll never be that Christ-like."

When you come across a weight you can't lift at the gym, you don't walk out – *you lessen it.* You do what you can and let your buddy spot you. Likewise, we must train on what God has given us the ability to do. His grace spots us when we fall short. "Turn the other cheek" means, don't return evil. I may not be able to resist striking someone who first struck me, but surely I can hold my tongue when someone curses me.

C. S. Lewis gave an example of another difficult principle of Christ: forgiveness. He said most agree that forgiveness sounds like a lovely idea, until we have something to forgive. Some may argue, for instance, how could a Jew forgive the Gestapo?

"When you start mathematics you do not begin with calculus; you begin with simple addition. In the same way, if we really want to learn how to forgive, perhaps we had better start with something easier than the Gestapo (C.S. Lewis, *Mere Christianity*)." Lewis suggests we first learn to forgive our wives, husbands, children, and co-workers before we jump to our enemies.

VEGGIE TALES

The term 'sleeping Christian' or the 'sleeping church' refers to an individual or group that needs to be awakened. But how long have we been asleep? Perhaps it's something more serious.

Having a loved one in a comatose state is heartbreaking. It's like they're there, but they're not. People will play songs, movies, or tell stories by their bedside, hoping that something will click – wishing that the person would miraculously become responsive.

The longer a person is comatose, the more likely they are to slip into a Persistent Vegetative State, or PVS. This is characterized by being awake but not aware. It's painfully deceptive. People may even seem like they're reacting to touch, light, or sound. But these are automatic behaviors that do not require brain function.

When a family finally decides to take a person off of life support, they have lost all hope. They have come to the conclusion that the heart may beat, but the soul, mind, and strength are gone. In reality, that person died a long time ago. But we only absorb the gravity of death when the heart stops.

The heart is the bare minimum requirement for life. Without loving God with our souls, our minds, and our strength, our faith is paralyzed. We're awake but not aware. Our reactions to sermons, worship, and testimonies are merely automatic behaviors.

Some of us live our entire lives on spiritual life support – fed directly from sermons. We've become a church of vegetables, completely incapable of becoming who Christ has called us to be. He patiently waits for us to be responsive, patiently waits for His sons and daughters to make a meaningful recovery. *Or are we already gone?*

Whether we keep the faith or not, pondering on what Jesus called the Greatest Commandments will give us perspective on what exactly we have made our god – if not Him. It's not about what we say we *love*, but what we *resemble*, what we *meditate on*, and what we will *persevere for*. We may find that we don't love Jesus; we only like Him.

LOVE: *The Great Omission*

There's a moment in my childhood that replays itself, perhaps for eternity. My parents and I were having lunch in downtown when a homeless man approached our table and begged for food. *My heart broke.* I asked my parents for a buck, and I handed it to him.

I promised myself that when I grew up, I would dedicate my entire life to street ministry — exemplifying Christ's love to beggars, drug addicts, and prostitutes.

I'm all grown up now, and I have dedicated *none* of my life to street ministry — I mean, they're just *beggars, drug addicts, and prostitutes!* And if one *ever* approached my table while I was enjoying my lunch, instead of giving him a dollar, I may be more inclined to give him *a piece of my mind!*

There's a moment in my adulthood that replays itself, perhaps for eternity. I was at BJ's Restaurant with my church family. As we were saying our goodbyes — which can take hours — a homeless man, who would have otherwise gone unnoticed, walks through our group grumbling epithets about our Ethiopian heritage. I don't remember exactly what he said, but it was in regards to us being 'African pirates' and 'stealing ships.'

I was infuriated! This idiot insulting us doesn't realize that 1) he's referring to Somalis (not that a Somalian would deserve that stereotypical assault), and 2) Ethiopia is a landlocked country (*how could we be pirates, you idiot?!*) But his desire to insult us was clear.

He couldn't detest me, because *I detest him first!* – that homeless bum! ***I saw red.*** Without hesitation, I grabbed the restaurant's promotional sign and approached him with the intention of pummeling his cranium! But before I could reach him, my friends tackled me — preventing me from hitting him with a 'piece' that would surpass his understanding!

What changed? When did I go from having compassion for the homeless, to detesting them? A small part of me still wanted to help — kind of. But if I haven't even exemplified Christ's love to my neighbors, co-workers, and associates, how then could I be an instrument of God, reaching out to those I now see as *detestable?*

When the prostitute was washing Jesus's feet, the Pharisees grumbled. To them, she was detestable prostitute – *a worthless being.* But to Jesus, she counted. Everyone who was overlooked and judged – from the Samaritan woman who had been divorced four times, to the woman about to be stoned for adultery – counted to Jesus.

The toughest part about being a Christian is understanding the value Christ has placed on people – *especially those we detest.* We don't have to be super religious to be Pharisees. All it takes is to think that we're better, that we're closer to God.

The Pharisees often grumbled about Jesus, saying, "This man receives sinners and eats with them" (Luke 15:2). To them, being close to God meant disassociating themselves from others. But Christ was a friend of sinners, He encouraged all to seek righteousness, with love. And He warned of those who "shut the door of the kingdom of heaven in people's faces" even though they themselves have not entered (Matthew 23:13-14).

BAD RELIGION

The Christian religion has been the source of so much division, anger, and death. It's obvious that so many adherents weren't truly disciples. *But are we?*

"Woe to you, teachers of the law and Pharisees, you hypocrites! You travel over land and sea to win a single convert, and when you have succeeded, you make them twice as much a child of hell as you are."
Matthew 23:15

In Jesus's day, the focus of religion was on rules and regulations. The Jews had over 600 laws – everything from, 'don't get a tattoo' to 'marry the woman you have raped.' It was hard to decipher between what was authentic faith and what was just bad religion.

The Pharisees were making followers of themselves, followers Jesus called 'children of hell'. And if these devout teachers of the law could be called out like this, it's got to make us ask ourselves, are we true disciples or merely the converts of Pharisees? Are we also children of hell?

The legalistic, rules-based mindset was carried over into Christianity as Gentile Christians were being pressured to obey Jewish laws – the main one being circumcision. These 'mutilators of the flesh', as the Apostle Paul called them, would make you feel like less of a believer if you didn't subscribe to their Biblical rules.

So the apostles came together, deciding that they should not make it burdensome for Gentiles to turn to God. After all, the fruits of the flesh are obvious (Galatians 5:19-21). They dropped the list down from 600 to four: "abstain from food sacrificed to idols, from blood, from the meat of strangled animals and from sexual immorality" (Acts 15:29). *But maybe this is just my interpretation.*

THE INTERPRETER

The Bible has empowered us, imperfect humans, with the ability to do *all things.* We can move mountains, be more than conquerors, but most importantly, we can use God's word out-of-context. We reshape it to match our personal interpretation, or *literal interpretation.* It allows us to perpetuate our own agenda with the good Lord's co-sign. Some of us have become the type of Pharisees that accused Jesus of breaking the literal rules – even once accusing Him of healing on the Sabbath!

We often name verses to support our objectives. After all, "If God is for us, then who can be against us?" (Romans 8:31). In essence, we've made God against somebody – somebody who may also think God is for them. Or worse, somebody who now – because of us – hates God. But it doesn't matter to us, because we're right! *The Bible says so.*

Once again, we find ourselves living to a standard that others aren't living to: *a Biblical standard.* But before we correct others, let's correct ourselves. Jesus said that the scribes and Pharisees – who lived to the highest standard–would "strain out a gnat and swallow a camel!" (Matthew 23:24) *He had quite the sense of humor.*

MAKING THE BAND

"If I speak in the tongues of men or of angels, but do not have love, I am only a resounding gong or a clanging cymbal." 1 Corinthians 13:1

What makes Christianity great is often the very element that is omitted –love. *The Great Commission* – Christ's command that the gospel be spread to the world – has become *The Great Omission.* For many, the Gospel is a clanging cymbal.

We can't even tell someone about Jesus because they already know – or think they do. Christianity has been spread across the globe much like a muddy mop has smeared across a floor. The mud – ambition, legalism, and hypocrisy –have tainted the Gospel.

The only regions that have been protected from our hypocrisy are regions that are under communism or Islamic law. It's in these places that we find the truest disciples. *Our comfort has become our curse.*

Many Christians represent God, but not love – which is impossible (1 John 4:8). Love is the true test of our faith. And not just love for people who share our faith. Our authenticity is evidenced by our love for God and neighbor, because anyone can say, "I'm a Christian."

THE BROAD OF CHRIST

"The Lord said to me, 'Go, show your love to your wife again, though she is loved by another man and is an adulteress. Love her as the Lord loves the Israelites, though they turn to other gods.'" Hosea 3:1

The chosen people went back and forth between idolatry and repentance, only returning to God in times of need. *Sound familiar?* To symbolize this unfaithfulness, God told Hosea to marry a prostitute.

Even after uniting in holy matrimony, Hosea's wife remained promiscuous. She even gave birth to a child that he suspected wasn't his. The story not only parallels our unfaithfulness to Jesus, but also suggests the fruit we bear may not be of His spirit.

The role of the Bride of Christ is to produce His fruit. But out of our unfaithfulness, we conceive fruits of the flesh – fruits that are obviously inconsistent with Christ's nature (Galatians 5:19-21). Our behavior brings mockery and shame, because it's no secret that *He is not the father.*

WHO'S THE DADDY?

Is there anything more humiliating than having a child that obviously isn't yours? We're talking *blatantly* not yours. Like, you and your wife are pale white, and this kid comes out chocolate. The delivery doctor can't even look you in the eyes as he asks, "Do you want to cut the umbilical cord?"

The illegitimacy would be no secret. In fact, you'd be the talk of the hospital break room. You may have been able to hide marital problems before, but this would be the dagger to your sacred union.

As a society, we're entertained by promiscuity. We've seen shows like *Maury*, in which, a woman brings her child and the potential fathers. In front of an audience, they try to determine whose child it may be, often comparing the baby's features to the men.

Not a single woman leaves the show with dignity. To the audience, they're morally bankrupt, even by the lenient standard of a secular world. In the end, the host opens an envelope and reads a lab result that identifies the biological father.

Anguish and grief befalls the man whose name is called. Simultaneously, the other men celebrate, claiming that they were confident that the results would vindicate them. In some instances, all of the men brought onto the show are cleared. It's an overwhelmingly shameful moment for the woman, but for the viewers, it's great entertainment!

Christians come under similar scrutiny, under the microscope of a secular audience. The fruit we have given birth to doesn't *resemble* who we claim is the Father. But God doesn't dance after hearing the lab results, boasting in laughter. As we're disgraced in the face of an unbelieving world, it gives them more reason to discredit our covenant with Jesus. Our spiritually adulterous nature is exposed to an audience of unbelievers, and they're entertained by our hypocrisy.

MYSTERY FRUIT

"By their fruit you will recognize them. Do people pick grapes from thorn bushes, or figs from thistles? Likewise, every good tree bears good fruit, but a bad tree bears bad fruit." Matthew 7:16-17

Can the same lips that bless be the same lips that curse? Can we be vessels of God and flesh, *a living contradiction?* If a good tree bears both good and bad fruit, it could be like a… mystery tree. Yeah, *that's it.* Enjoy a delightful snack, *or* get poisoned and die. Ahh, the thrill in uncertain expectation. *Bon appétit!*

How would you rate a restaurant that serves very delicious entrees, *but* frequently causes food poisoning? Is it both good and bad? Cut it some slack. After all, it was mighty tasty! *Don't be an absolutist,* writing it off just because of a little diarrhea, colon inflammation, and projectile vomiting. What about the good times when you left the establishment with dignity, without falling to your knees and repenting over the toilet?

Let's say you're the restaurant owner. You have identified the chef who is responsible for these delicious, yet deadly meals. Is he a good or bad employee? He's only human! Cut him some slack! If you advise him of his fault, he may remind you of his tasty dishes and perhaps even prepare you something special!

If the chef continues to drive customers away – either to competition or the mortuary – you may have to fire him. He's a bad employee. *You absolutist.* You take back his uniform and access card so he doesn't misuse it. The last thing you need is for him to pose as your own.

Christians are called to be actively working, bearing fruit for the kingdom. But we produce both good and bad fruits, oftentimes poisoning others. Instead of confronting our faults, we boast in our good works! We remind God that we resisted temptation or did a good deed, as if it were a meaningful rebuttal.

Jesus told us to abide in Him so that we would bear His fruit, otherwise be cut off (John 15:2). Maybe we're not of God's kingdom; *maybe we're just wearing the uniform.*

Time and time again, we return to Christ to once again be His bride. But we've been down this road before. The spirit is willing, but flesh is weak. We love Jesus; we love sin. It's evident that we have a glaring conflict of interest.

PART 4:
CONFLICT (OF INTEREST) RESOLUTION

THE CASE FOR COMPROMISE

I hope my interjections have been helping you so far. But in this chapter, I would like to go in depth, and address our conflict of interest with a case for compromise.

"Put on the full armor of God, so that you can take your stand against the devil's schemes." Ephesians 6:11

Paul the Apostle encourages us to put on the full armor of God. He stresses the belt of truth, shield of faith, and yada yada yada. Paul's letter is clearly outdated. We need a more practical solution, a solution for the modern day Comfortable Christian. Let's ease the spiritual battle Paul seems to think we are fighting. Why be bogged down with all the "armor"? Why "stand against the devil's schemes" if we can cut a deal? After all, why is he scheming against us in the first place? *Let's call a truce!*

CONQUERING AIN'T EASY

Sure, we love Bible verses that say we are more than conquerors. But there's a time for war, and there's a time for peace. We don't want to be conquering *all* of the time. Give it a rest! Conquering ain't easy. And it's ease, not victory, that most of us are aiming for.

As Comfortable Christians, we must stay off of the devil's radar. *Stealth is key.* Every gamer knows that he's less likely to be attacked if he's not moving. The key, then, is to stay still and do nothing while the enemy attacks our teammates. The enemy's chances of finding us are drastically reduced, although not completely ruled out.

In these virtual online battlefields, we sometimes come across an enemy that isn't moving. They are either, a) away from their game console, b) have a bad Internet connection and can't move with fluidity, or c) have a strategy to stay still to not get attacked. They want to be on the team, but don't want to fight. *Ahh, the cyber peace-loving hippie!*

So what happens if the enemy finds us not moving? Well, in games like *Halo*, they may punch us a bit to see if we're responsive. *Our screen blinks red.* Now we have a choice to make. We can, a) spring to life and attack (which may attract attention from more enemies), or b) remain calm, do nothing, and hope that the enemy doesn't kill us. After all, they get more satisfaction from killing a moving target. If we do get killed, *it's okay.* In seconds we'll re-spawn –hopefully close to a better hiding spot.

There are three reasons why a Christian is not on the enemy's radar. We're either, a) completely away from God, b) have a bad connection with Him and can't move with fluidity, or c) our strategy is to not get attacked. We want to be on the team, but don't want to fight. If we're not a threat to the devil, then the devil shouldn't be a threat to us, *right?*

PROVOKING THE ENEMY

Nehemiah told the people of Israel, who were comfortably living within the city's ruined walls, of God's plan to rebuild. As they began to progress, enemies rose up in opposition. *You see,* Nehemiah provoked them! *Instigator!* If he had just been comfortable with Jerusalem's demolished status, they wouldn't have been confronted by this threat. After all, the enemy wasn't against their plan, *but against God's.*

Sure, the wall was completed, fulfilling God's plan for him and the people of Israel, but *not without resistance!* As Comfortable Christians, we must keep in mind that the act of enduring anything is a threat to our identity. We can learn from Nehemiah's mistake and avoid provoking the enemy by being content with our spiritually demolished state.

In effect, we neutralize the enemy by neutralizing ourselves first, robbing our would-be attackers of the incentive to fight us. Liken it to playing dead while a battle rages around us: *our only risk is being stepped on!* It's only when we're *rudely* tearing down the devil's work that he attacks us in self-defense! So let's take a timeout. Surely we can forge some kind of compromise.

THE ART OF COMPROMISE

Chances are, if we aren't being attacked by the devil's schemes, a compromise has already been made. As tool of the flesh, compromise works in the background, *lobbying for carnal interests.* Coupled with a lack of transparency in self-reflection, compromising prevents our spirits from being alarmed by gradual concession.

"All compromise is based on give and take, but there can be no give and take on fundamentals. Any compromise on mere fundamentals is surrender. For it is all give and no take." -Mahatma Gandhi

I beg to differ. Compromising effectively is all about learning to rationalize. For example, many Christians listen to music that is filled with a message of sex, partying, and drugs. We fill our minds with stuff that directly contradicts our faith. At a glance, this makes no sense. But wait, we like the beat. And maybe there isn't enough Christian music out there. Maybe we can take comfort knowing that other Christians are listening to it also... just not to and from church. *Excellent rationale.*

Let's say a Klansman likes grooving to the harmonious sounds of Snoop Dogg & Dr. Dre. At a glance, the two are in absolute conflict! There's not much that they agree on, aside from the liberal use of the n-word. So how can a Klansman rationalize listening to gangster rap? Well, maybe he likes the beat. Maybe there isn't enough good Klan rap out there. Maybe he knows of other Klansmen who also enjoy hip-hop… just not to and from cross burnings. *Excellent rationale.*

This method can also be used to justify other sticky issues like 'reading' the *Sports Illustrated Swimsuit Issue*. It's not porn, so it's technically okay. *C'mon,* we live in a hyper-sexualized society! We can't even buy groceries without learning 'tips to make your man go wild in bed.' Most importantly, rationale allows us to justify ungodly relationships, ungodly environments, and a love affair with garbage media.

WALKING THE TIGHTROPE

We can even use the word of God to support our compromising stance. Jesus stated that, "It's not what goes into a man that defiles him, but what comes out" (Matthew 15:11). That means we can enjoy secular music, junk media, and almost-porn magazines, as long as we don't let these things influence our desires, *right?*

In fact, we build up a tolerance of sorts. Sure, an inexperienced Comfortable Christian may falter in his walk upon stumbling across suggestive content. But to the *seared conscience* (cough, cough) I mean, to the one *mature* in the ways of Comfortable Christianity, he will be seasoned enough to endure the temptation.

Temptation leads to sin, but technically, the thought itself, is not sin. So why not *enjoy* (cough, cough) I mean, why not *endure* the temptation? Some hardliners would argue that if you let a temptation linger, then you might eventually succumb to it. But why be so pessimistic? *The keg is half full.*

The Bible has stories of people who didn't compromise, and probably *lived* to regret it. Take Joseph for example – his brothers sold him into slavery. Despite losing everything, he held on to God and found favor with the chief of Pharaoh's guard, Potiphar, – *and Potiphar's wife.*

Taking into consideration that Potiphar was one of the highest-ranking officials, *he probably had a trophy wife.* In fact, she may have been one of *the hottest* chicks in Egypt! After trying to seduce Joseph to no avail, she finally stripped off his clothes. This is clearly a special circumstance that falls under the 'Tempted beyond what you can bear' clause, detailed in 1 Corinthians 10:13. In addition, she was his superior and he was just a mere servant. What about that verse that says, "Servants, obey your masters"? (Ephesians 6:5). Joseph could have exercised either of these exceptions, but instead, he ran from temptation! Angrily, she accused him of rape, and he was subsequently thrown in jail. So much for being rewarded for perseverance (James 1:12).

Imagine having to explain that your crime was *refusing* the advances of Potiphar's supermodel wife, *to your rapist cellmate.* Instead of just banking on God's forgiveness, you have become the laughing stock of the prison yard.

Sure, God rewarded his faithfulness and made him second command in Egypt and he was reunited with his family – blah blah blah. Don't miss the bigger point: He missed out on Potiphar's wife! We may not fulfill God's plan for our lives if we're compromising, *but dang,* she was fine!

Jesus is strong when our flesh is weak. In fact, the Apostle Paul said that he "boasts in his weaknesses" (2 Corinthians 12:9). What I'm advocating for is more weaknesses for more boasting.

NO REGRETS

Scratching something off of your *bucket list* refers to the concept that you have completed something you wanted to do before you die – like running a marathon, or even shark diving. Order is of great of importance, as shark diving could adversely affect your ability to run a marathon. Nonetheless, the idea is that the fulfillment of these goals would make our lives feel complete. Then we can die, *comfortably.*

Ideally, when it's all said and done, we would like to look back at our lives and die with no regrets. Meaning, it'd be nice to reach a point when we can accept death and be comfortable with it. We've done everything that we wanted to – we've lived a fulfilled life. If the grim reaper came knocking, we'd have no complaints. But after we die, does it make any difference to us – the dead people – that we completed our bucket list? If not, what's the point of a fulfilled life? Why not just die now?

We don't want to die today because we would regret so much. The very regrets that we don't want to have are what keep us alive – they're our driving force. We live to regret.

Wait, what?

If we want to be rich, we regret being poor. If we want a family, we regret being single. If we want to be productive, we regret wasting time. Without regret, we would have nothing to push for. But we don't realize just how much we regret, until we're faced with death.

"It is better to go to a house of mourning than to go to a house of feasting, for death is the destiny of everyone; the living should take this to heart." Ecclesiastes 7:2

Let's suppose that today you were mugged at gunpoint. You're shaking and overwhelmed with fear (presuming that this was not on your bucket list). You think to yourself, "I don't want to die." But why not? Maybe there are things you wanted to do, like get married, raise kids or grandkids. *Regrets*. Maybe you will regret not being able to tell a loved one goodbye. Whatever it is, will you regret not being able to do all those things from your grave?

Bang. You've been shot in an alley. This is not the way or time you planned on dying. You think of your friends, your family, your... *nothing.* You fade to black. Death just set you free from all those regrets, goals, and burdens.

A COMFORTABLE DEATH

"Those who belong to Christ Jesus have crucified the flesh with its passions and desires." Galatians 5:24

We don't want to die to our flesh just yet. After all, we may *eternally regret* not fulfilling our desires! Imagine the despair of being in heaven, but all you can think about is the stuff you missed out on. *Oh my gods!* Especially if we know people who have lived it up and are now back with Jesus. Okay, so it's not that blatant. But we want to enjoy our lives to an extent.

Are there particular bucket list items that we can do that will make our flesh comfortable with dying? Or would that just increase its hunger? Perhaps 'death to self' would in itself set us free from that regret.

We're all familiar with the cliché movie scene in which someone pleads, "But I'm too young to die." I think it's safe to say that it's a rather ineffectual rebuttal. Either way, the person facing death insists that he still has so much to live for. He didn't have a full life.

Truth is, even if we lived a full life, at the end we may still wish we could live forever. Obviously, not in our old, wrinkled, and crippled state. After all, what's the use of being immortal if you have been reduced to memory loss, hearing aids, and diapers?

If somehow we could reverse the aging, we would want to live forever. We long to be young again, to keep carrying out our passions and desires.

SOMEBODY'S GOTTA DIE

We're in a constant struggle. We regret that if we indulge in sin, we're failing to strengthen our spirit. We often try to appease both, but there's no compromise. It's better to be hot or cold than to be lukewarm. Spiritually, it's either death or dishonor. Ultimately, when we try to save both, we lose both.

Somebody's gotta die. The casualty will either be our flesh, or our spirit and flesh. *Wait, what?* You see, our flesh is going to die anyway, but misery loves company. We've all observed yet another cliché movie scene in which someone is shot and dying, but bravely tells his friend to go on without him – to save himself. Never does the wounded man say, "Don't leave ... let's both be gunned down."

But that's exactly what the flesh does!

Every day it's dying, and sometimes death is sudden. Through Christ, we seek eternal life. But our flesh is pleading with our spirit, "Don't leave, let's both die." Trying to save the flesh is a lost cause.

THE LOST CAUSE

"The Spirit gives life; the flesh counts for nothing. The words I have spoken to you – they are full of the Spirit and life. Yet there are some of you who do not believe." John 6:63-64

By definition, a lost cause is a cause with no chance of success, a losing campaign. Oftentimes, we're heavily invested in it, making it hard to quit. We feel that if we just invest a bit more, we can reach success.

For example, some say the *War on Drugs* is a lost cause. For decades, the United States has spent billions to fight it, while remaining the world's largest consumer. Some seek to end the war, citing its ineffectiveness and cost. Others disagree, citing it as a need to step up enforcement. Ultimately, our effort may count for nothing.

Our fleshly desires are insatiable; we'll always want more, no matter what we have. Scrooge McDuck will always want more gold; the Cookie Monster will always want more cookies. Consider Halle Berry, who is regarded as one of the most beautiful women in the world. Even her beauty wasn't enough to quench the insatiable desire of her former cheating husband, Eric Benet.

"'And what does pleasure accomplish?' I tried cheering myself with wine, and embracing folly-my mind still guiding me with wisdom. I wanted to see what was good for people to do under the heavens during the few days of their lives." Ecclesiastes 2:2-3

Seeking to satisfy the desires of our flesh is a losing campaign. It accomplishes nothing. We can either continue to pour into it, intentionally blinding ourselves to the inevitable loss, or we can kill it now.

BLAZE OF GLORY

"Or don't you know that all of us who were baptized into Christ Jesus were baptized into his death?" Romans 6:3

Everyone will die. We picture ourselves old and gray, dying peacefully in our sleep — of natural causes. For some reason, we all expect to get so old we don't want to live anymore. Not only is that boring; it's not promised. Why wait, when we can go out in a blaze of glory?

Envision yourself live on television, jumping a flaming motorcycle from rooftop to rooftop. Cheers turn into shrieks as you slightly miscalculate. Or imagine being a soldier of the Allied Forces in World War II – your heroic invasion of Normandy is welcomed by a hail of Nazi bullets. One, of course, is more honorable than the other, depending on: a) whether your definition of a hero is a war veteran or an X-games contestant, or b) if the bike was a Harley-Davidson. The only thing that can top both, is storming the shores of Normandy *on* a flaming Harley-Davidson! (Still to be gunned down by Nazis). *YES!* Now that is the way to go.

"We were therefore buried with him through baptism into death in order that, just as Christ was raised from the dead through the glory of the Father, we too may live a new life." Romans 6:4

When we crucify the flesh, we're *resurrected* in a blaze of glory, *His glory*. Our friends, family, and co-workers will witness the dramatic change in our lives. Our legacy will no longer be of the former things, but of His righteousness. They see our good deeds, and glorify God (Matthew 5:16). If there was ever a cause to die for, a glorious cause, it's Christ.

THE CIRCLE OF LIFE

"Very truly I tell you, unless a kernel of wheat falls to the ground and dies, it remains only a single seed. But if it dies, it produces many seeds." John 12:24

When the purpose of a seed comes into fruition, it produces many seeds. This of course, can only happen if it dies. What if the seed didn't want to die? Perhaps it felt like it was missing out on life, which ultimately led to missing out on its purpose.

If we, Christians, are not producing other Christians through the fruit of the Spirit, then we have lost our purpose. It's the unwillingness to die to self. After all, we're too young to die; we have so much to regret.

PRODIGAL PROSPECTS

We all love a good testimony, and by good testimony, we mean the story of a former life full of sex, drugs, and alcohol. *Maybe even violence!* Hallelujah! It's so inspirational, so uplifting to know that God can save us from all that fun. *Yes,* fun.

As a testimony reaches its climax, seemingly peaking in the indulgence of earthly pleasures, it's curbed with a *sigh.* "Is this it, is this all the world has to offer?" The realization of its emptiness sets in ... and like a script, it's God's queue.

The congregation listens intently in awe, amazed at what God brought him/her out of. They can never look at you the same. Wide eyes question, *"You had sex with how many men/women?!"* or, *"You sold how much dope?!"* Some wonder what it would be like to experience the *dark side* and still get to be saved. For a moment, we live vicariously through their testimony – *or at least I did.* It sounded like they had their cake and ate it too. Now, I could never *completely* reject Jesus and dive into the pool of earthly pleasures, but I wanted to get my feet wet.

Let's consider the people who clung to Jesus in their youth. How un-awesome is their testimony? *We don't even call it a testimony!* There's no sex, no drugs, no alcohol. It's flat out boring.

The *now redeemed* Christians who have experienced sex, drugs, and alcohol are just as saved as the square Christians who've only dreamed about it. And they don't get the *slightest* praise. There's less mystique, and more perplexed looks when our wide eyes question, *"Wait... you're still a virgin, bro?"*

REDEMPTION SONG

We're all familiar with the *Parable of the Prodigal Son*. The parable demonstrates God's compassion and desire to see the rebellious return. There were two brothers, one of whom asks the father for his inheritance in advance. He squanders it on hookers, parties, and extravagance. He lived the life of a rock-star.

Then a famine hit the land. Broke and starving, he found a job feeding pigs. In his hunger, he broke down and ate with them. Disgusted with himself, he decided to return home – not as a son, *but perhaps as a servant.*

His father, seeing him a long way off, rushed to greet him. Immediately, he threw his son a party. But the good brother was irked by this glorious redemption. He was jealous that his brother could have all that fun, waste half of the family fortune, and still be considered a son – *just like him.* It wasn't fair. While he was sowing seeds, his brother was sowing royal oats!

The twist in the story is when the famine hits and all of his money – his father's resource – is gone. When pleasure proves itself to be empty, or to have run out, we question ourselves. Have we made our purpose the indulgence of the senses?

Consider those moments we think "This… this is what life is all about!" Usually, our *senses* reaffirm us. My taste buds have supported the notion many-a-time while carving off juicy morsels of medium-rare rib-eye steak. "This… this is what life is all about! *Gluttony!*"

How much of our Father's resource – our lives – have we wasted on pleasure? Would we even search for Him if things remained smooth sailing, or are we waiting for the low moment? Either way, He celebrates our return.

Grace is a cornerstone and stumbling stone. It doesn't change the fact that, well, we don't want to miss out on pleasure. We want the best of both worlds, heaven and earth.

 Earth is a limited time offer, so get it out of your system now. Because once we get to heaven there won't be any sex, drugs, or alcohol. We'll eternally sing old English hymns – regardless of linguistic preference.

NO FAIR

"Whoever tries to keep their life will lose it, and whoever loses their life will preserve it." Luke 17:33

If we have recognized that our life is a resource granted to us by the Father, wouldn't we manage it, as opposed to taking ownership? When we take ownership, we find it difficult to do the smallest things for Him. Everything is a task – *a task that the Lord better take note of!* Especially if we've recently made a prayer request.

One of the first words babies mouth out is, "ma-ma." We think it's sweet, failing to see that these selfish mini-ingrates are trying to say, "ma-*mine!*" Every object given to them is "ma-*mine!*" This sense of ownership is rooted in our nature. We seek to preserve what we have – *especially if we deem it to be little.*

In the *Parable of the Talents*, Jesus compared our lives to that of servants who have been given coins to invest. Some were given more than others. The servant who was given only one coin buried it, fearing that he didn't have much to begin with. *This upset the master.* The coin, as insignificant as it seemed, was meant to be invested.

"Whoever has will be given more; whoever does not have, even what they have will be taken from them." Mark 4:25

At first glance, it may seem like Saint Mark is citing *The Wall Street Journal*. And since we love to pick bits of scripture that would serve our purposes, I find it alarming that this verse isn't the slogan of the New York Stock Exchange. After all, no portfolio is complete without a dividend that yields moral highground.

How is this principle fair, Jesus? Everyone knows that it takes money to make money. Is that fair? No, it's just reality.

Clinging to the concept of fairness is a disadvantage. It's an immature concept, one that's reinforced in grade school. Perhaps our educators could have better prepared us – maybe by randomly giving some of us harder tests than others.

Our Father, unlike us, doesn't judge on the raw material, but on what has been done with it. For example, our social decency is often a product of our upbringing. Depending on what we've made of it, we could be morally worse than those we regard as fiends. This is precisely why Jesus said that prostitutes and tax collectors – those regarded as fiends – will enter the kingdom before (seemingly devout, and socially respectable) Pharisees.

"Most of the man's psychological make-up is probably due to his body: when his body dies all that will fall off him, and the real central man, the thing that chose, that made the best or the worst out of this material, will stand naked." -C.S. Lewis

WAITING IN VAIN

Imagine being the prodigal son. You come home to find your brother hadn't done anything – *aside from self-righteously complain about you.* Sure he, the good son, stayed home, but only to wait on his inheritance.

The point of Christianity isn't to go to church and wait for eternal life. If this is what we have done with our material, our faith, then we have wasted just as much time *if not more* than the rebellious. Potentially, we may be waiting in vain.

Just because we haven't forsaken God in hot pursuit of sensual indulgence doesn't mean we're any better than those who have. If we have nothing to account for our relationship with our Father, then we too, have buried the talent in the ground. The prodigal children may one day see the futility of making carnal pleasure a purpose, but we're in danger because we fancy ourselves the good sons and daughters.

GET RIGHTEOUS OR DIE TRYING

In an attempt to trap Jesus, the Pharisees asked whether it was right to pay taxes to Caesar. It was a controversial question, because the Jews were seeking a messiah to deliver them from Roman rule. The answer 'yes' would turn people away; the answer 'no' would get Him in trouble. His reply? "Show me a coin."

"And he asked them, 'Whose image is this? And whose inscription?' 'Caesar's,' they replied. Then he said to them, 'So give back to Caesar what is Caesar's, and to God what is God's.'" Matthew 22:20-21

Our greatest conflict of interest, where many of us struggle the most, is right here. Jesus doesn't consider money important, but we give it the utmost importance. Even as believers, we misplace our priorities.

I never cared much for people who answer a question with a question. *And Jesus was the king of this* (not that He isn't the king of basically everything). His question, "Whose image is this?" really asks, "Whose image are you?"

The money was made in Caesar's image; we're made in God's image. Caesar gave the coin value; our Creator gave us value. Despite this truth, we often give ourselves not to God, but to money – *chasing it becomes our identity.*

 As awesome as it sounds that God values us, the tragic irony is that He values our irritating neighbors as well.

Jesus wants us to stop being slaves to material, to find our purpose by giving ourselves back to Him. Our bodies are temples. The question is, for whom? Are we temples of Christ, *or Caesar's palace?*

VANTAGE POINT

The Christian worldview envisions human purpose within the human Source. All things are from Him, through Him, and for Him (Romans 11:36). It's a very humble worldview, *in theory.* The ultimate hope is that we can fellowship with Him, if indeed He has given us a path to do so.

"For there is one God and one mediator between God and mankind, the man Christ Jesus, who gave himself as a ransom for all people." 1 Timothy 2: 5-6

The hope is rooted in Jesus's claim to be the Way, the Truth, and Life – that no one reaches the Father but by Him (John 14:6). He told us to seek and we will find, knock and the door would be opened (Matthew 7:7).

Even among those with a Christian worldview, the search for purpose usually focuses on the right career, the right relationship, or a fulfilling hobby. But consider Adam, who walked and talked with God everyday before sin separated them. When he was cast out of the Garden of Eden, a spiritual realm, he had to make a living by the sweat of his brow (Genesis 3:19).

Picture Adam trying to find purpose in the sweat of his brow! Perhaps being a farmer or hunter-gatherer didn't *fulfill* him like fishing did. Obviously, no occupation could give him greater purpose than reconnecting with his Source. So why do we search for our purpose in occupation? Sure, finding a job that we like is important, but it's only secondary to spiritual redemption.

RAGS TO RIGHTEOUSNESS

"And all of our righteous acts are like filthy rags; we all shrivel up like a leaf, and like the wind our sins sweep us away." Isaiah 64:6

This world seeks purpose in success, which is often valued in money, power, and sex. The rapper 50 Cent made his purpose clear, as it was the title of his debut album, *Get Rich or Die Trying*. Society may not chant this mantra, but it's the mainstream ideology pertaining to purpose. Theoretically, it would be better for Mr. 50 Cent to die than to stop trying to get rich.

Sure he had other things aside from riches that he sought to fulfill himself with, like women, power, and influence. But his priorities were clear, *money above all*. He sought first his own kingdom, and all else followed.

"Homie, you hustlin' backwards if you chasing a [woman], chase the paper they come with the [stuff]." -50 Cent

As Christians, our priority should be clear, 'get righteous or die trying.' It would be better for us to die than to stop seeking God. We're 'hustlin' backwards' if our search for fulfillment on earth is greater than our search for God. We'll never reach our purpose if we're preoccupied with what to wear, where to work, and who to date.

HOUSE RULES

"But seek first his kingdom and his righteousness, and all these things will be given to you as well." Matthew 6:33

We don't like the idea of putting all of our eggs in one basket — a basket, one might add, that's intangible. So we diversify the portfolio. We invest ourselves in what we deem to be worthwhile.

Where exactly do our investments lie? And if, or when they fall apart, what then? Let's say we don't get the promotion that we expected, a close relationship ends, or we lose our material possessions. *What then?*

Investing is synonymous to gambling, depending on the level of knowledge of the investor, or gambler. Even with knowledge, the market or game can be volatile; the odds may not be in our favor. But the broker always wins because their fee is not based on our success, and the house always gets a cut of every hand dealt.

The world will always get the best of us if we invest in what it has to offer. And all of its offerings lose value. *So why invest in something that loses value?* Once we drive a new car off the lot, it loses value. Weddings may cost tens of thousands of dollars, yet half of marriages end in divorce – loss of value. No one can ever forget the way Justin Timberlake cried when his house, cars, and furniture were being repossessed on the celebrity prank show, *Punk'd.* What happens when all we have invested in is lost, and Ashton Kutcher isn't there to tell us it's going to be okay?

"The kingdom of heaven is like a treasure hidden in a field. When a man found it, he hid it again, and then in his joy went and sold all he had and bought that field." Matthew 13:44

The man in the parable realized that nothing he owned or could hope to own was worth the treasure. He probably didn't waste time trying to get the market value on his belongings – it was nothing in comparison. But it's not *all* nothing, is it? That reluctance we have, our lust for possessions, makes us weigh whether our kingdom is worth giving up for God's.

POSSESSED BY POSSESSIONS

"Whoever loves money never has enough; whoever loves wealth is never satisfied with their income. This too is meaningless." Ecclesiastes 5:10

We've all heard about what money can and cannot buy. Money can buy a bed, but not rest. Money can buy the best medical care, but not health. Money can buy sex, but not love. Nevertheless, this cliché proverb doesn't quell our desire for more money.

At one point or another, we've all wished that we could *just be rich*, and the rich wish they could *just be richer*. Money can't buy happiness, *so we've been told.* Many people who have had great success are still empty inside, especially if they reach a point where they have exhausted pleasure. *Maybe they need more success.* Our lives are dedicated to chasing either our Source or a sense of accomplishment, depending on our worldview.

King Solomon had the *winning trifecta* of success and happiness: wisdom, wealth, and women. With a collection of 700 wives, he must have celebrated, on average, two anniversaries a night! He had an unquenchable sexual appetite, a thirst for sensuality that didn't require the aid of male enhancement. Yet he wrote what could be considered the most depressing book in the Bible, *Ecclesiastes*. He exhausted pleasure.

Despite his status, material wealth, and assorted variety of sexual companions, he concluded that they were all meaningless because he forsook his purpose in God. There's no joy in pursuing happiness, *just more pursuit.* He warned us, who will most likely have significantly less, not to do the same.

In college, my Economics teacher began his first lecture by explaining to us that the sexiest word in the English language was 'insatiable.' He explained that our insatiable desires make the luxuries we already own feel like nothing. This is why we don't see ourselves as rich. Our insatiable desire blinds us to the fact that we have so much more than the vast majority of the world. And because we have more, it's even harder to give it up.

People often say, "I just want to be happy," ever failing to realize that chasing happiness can be an addiction. We will always want more, and it usually takes more. As kids, the smallest things made us happy – like a silly face. We get older, and it takes toys, clothes, or a relationship. Some briefly find happiness in marriage, but then need to 'spice things up' with their spouse, *or without their spouse.* Our careers don't make us happy; we need a higher position or salary. We need more of everything.

In addition, the circumstance that facilitates our happiness may also facilitate someone else's sadness. If you get promoted at your job, your co-worker didn't. You're happy, he's sad. If you lose an important game, you're sad; your opponent is happy. America was founded on the right to life, liberty, and the pursuit of happiness! But whose happiness are we talking about – Thomas Jefferson's or Kunta Kente's?

Instead of pursuing happiness, we should pursue joy. Happiness is circumstantial; it's at the mercy of our current situation. It's emotional and temporary. But joy is un-circumstantial, lasting, and a fruit of the Spirit – *a fruit of our Source.*

If we're not born of the Spirit, then we seek happiness; it's a never-ending pursuit. True fulfillment is found in righteousness, in loving God and neighbor. The Apostle Paul, a well-educated man with a promising career, reduced himself to work as tent-maker. He wrote, "I count all things to be loss in the view of the surpassing value of knowing Christ Jesus my Lord" (Philippians 3:8). As we ponder the big decisions in our lives – what career we choose, who we get into a relationship with, and what to eat for lunch – let's not forget how much more important it is to seek Jesus daily, in all things.

LOSING PURPOSE

The Christian faith has over two billion adherents, all who hope to one day hear the words, "Well done, good and faithful servant" — *despite whether they were good or faithful servants.* Where's this workforce in the field? If nearly ⅓ of the world's population are servants of Christ, shouldn't the other ⅔ be transformed by Christ's purpose? Truth is, most of us have called in sick, are absent without leave, or have been in orientation for years.

This isn't a call to action, to get out and convert others; *it's a call to convert ourselves.* Can a drowning man throw another drowning man a rope? *Sure,* if they intend to share it on the ocean floor. Likewise, we can only convince people to hold on to Jesus if they're fine with His purpose being neither visible nor practical.

SELLING JESUS

Much to their dismay, salesmen are rarely reciprocated the same enthusiasm they engage people with. Not many eagerly anticipate means by which they can rid themselves of hard-earned cash. And rarely do people want to be persuaded that they need a product to make their lives better.

There are three main types of salesman, the first category being the *Cold-Caller.* This group consists of telemarketers, door-to-door salesmen, and e-mail spammers. Their success hinges on our level of glee upon opening the door to a complete stranger, answering a phone number we don't recognize, or responding to sketchy e-mail.

Cold-Caller
TARGET CONSUMER: Everybody.
STRATEGY: Harass everybody. Somebody will like it.

The second category is the *Counter Representative*. This group is usually stationed at a mall, calling out to people who are shopping for other stuff. They're somewhat successful, depending on their personality.

Counter Representative
TARGET CONSUMER: Everybody ready to buy other stuff.
STRATEGY: Harass everybody ready to buy other stuff.

Thirdly, there is the *In-Store Representative*, and they have the most success. We've either come into their store or called their number to potentially buy what they have. We'll listen to them as they try to persuade us to buy more. *Cha-Ching!*

In-Store Representative
TARGET CONSUMER: Somebody looking to buy their stuff.
STRATEGY: Harass them into buying more stuff than they had planned to.

So what type of salespeople are we for Jesus: a) the *Cold-Caller*, who tells everyone they're Christian, b) the *Counter Rep*, who reaches out to all who are looking for something else, or c) the *In-Store Rep*, who has found someone receptive to Jesus, then overloads them with our doctrine?

Let's be none of them! Let's first focus on exemplifying Christ, not selling religion.

"And whatever you do, whether in word or deed, do it all in the name of the Lord Jesus, giving thanks to God the Father through him." Colossians 3:17

If we said and did everything in Jesus's name, it would be impossible to do things that are not of Him. *Road rage*, in Jesus's name? *Gossip*, in Jesus's name? *Idolatry, dishonesty, drunkenness...* in Jesus's name? If our speech, our jobs, the way we carry ourselves were all done to glorify God, then He would shine through our lives. This doesn't negate our duty to witness, but rather to be aware that our actions are a louder witness.

When something sells itself, it does so because its value is obvious, meaningful, and productive. Oftentimes, the consumer is the one who inquires because he/she sees how well it's working for someone else. If we truly had Jesus, wouldn't our lives be a testament to His value? Theoretically, it would develop an interest. *Theoretically.*

Sometimes our friends offer us things that haven't worked for them. Let's say a friend swore by a particular diet, *but he's becoming obese.* Or perhaps another recommended a foreign skin cream, *but she's developing rashes.* You don't knock your friends for trying to help, but since it isn't working for them, then it probably isn't going to work for you.

Most likely, our friends, classmates, and co-workers know that we're Christian. So from their perspective, "Is Jesus working out for us?" Or is something that's supposed to produce righteousness, producing self-righteousness? Is something that's supposed to produce love, producing hate? They may not be knocking us for it, but Jesus's value may not be obvious, meaningful, or productive.

REVIEWS, REFERRALS, TESTIMONIALS

Few people trust salesmen, but we generally trust third-party reviews. Why? Because salesmen – as friendly as some may be – *might not* have our best interests in mind. On the other hand, we like reviews, referrals, and testimonials because they're more likely to offer unbiased opinions.

For example, we may check *Rotten Tomatoes,* a movie review website, to determine if we should watch a film. After all, every movie commercial makes it look like *this* movie is the best movie. They show the best scenes on the trailer and post selected quotes along the lines of, "#1 Comedy of the week." But there's only one comedy out this week.

Let's say a highly anticipated film received poor reviews. Who do we trust: the testimonials or advertisements? If we go anyway, maybe because our favorite actor is in it, we may find that the best parts were in the commercial. Oftentimes, the best a movie has to offer is the trailer.

Is the best part of our faith in the commercial? Is all we have, "God loves you?" Do we fail to live up to the hype? If someone, somehow, is still drawn in by Jesus, let's not prove the bad reviews.

THE MISSION STATEMENT

A mission statement describes the purpose of an organization, company, or group. It states the main objective for its existence. It's the framework that an organization uses to guide its actions and reach its goals. It needs to address three things:

a) the target market,
b) the contribution it plans to make, and
c) what distinguishes it from other competing organizations.

Let's say we opened a lemonade stand in an already refreshment-saturated market. We name it *Cash Money, Young Money Lemonade.* Our objective can't be: make cash money selling lemonade. If it is, then we might cut corners, like possibly watering-down the product to increase profitability. Lemonade connoisseurs might not appreciate this and ultimately turn to another refreshment source. Our contribution isn't special, and we may lose business and harm our reputation.

Christ's mission was clear:
Target Market: *People with ears.* "Whoever has ears, let him hear" (Matthew 11:15). *Figuratively, deaf not excluded.*

Contribution: *Wholeness.* "I have come that they may have life, and have it to the full" (John 10:10). *Not material wealth, as His kingdom is not of this world.*

Distinguishing Factor: *He's the only way to the Father.* "I am the way and the truth and the life. No one comes to the Father except through me" (John 14:6).

Instead of disciplining our mission after His, we often forget that there's a mission in the first place. We find ourselves just *winging it* – a vague framework that misguides our actions and goals. This leads to cutting corners, making the 'life of wholeness' that we speak of, indistinguishable when compared to the lives of unbelievers. Consider how our rates of divorce, substance abuse, and debt rival that of the irreligious.

Does Jesus have any practical use in our lives? Perhaps we've watered-down the product, making it easier for us to peddle. But for connoisseurs of purity, it's a load of crap.

For example, let's use a problem that transcends worldviews: divorce. Imagine if there was little to no divorce in the church. In an age where over half of marriages fail, people would have taken notice. It would spark, at the very least, curiosity – especially now that people are losing faith in monogamy. We'd be a light to the world, a light that's obvious, meaningful, and productive.

Instead of reflecting Jesus, we often reflect our surroundings. *What does the world expect?* We're just regular Christians.

REGULAR CHRISTIANS

Since there's nothing regular about Christ, there shouldn't be anything regular about His followers. In fact, He called us to do greater things than He did. But rarely, if ever, do we envision ourselves ministering, healing, or delivering. If we downplay God's ability to use us, we downplay our mission — potentially to the point where we lose purpose.

Picture yourself as a chosen agent of *Seal Team 6*, the special operations unit dispatched onto Osama Bin Laden's back porch. As you hit the ground, you begin downplaying your eligibility. You question your training – simulations are basically video games! *This is real.* In lieu of bringing justice to the international terrorist, you find yourself climbing back into the helicopter, tending to the poppy garden, or even taking a dip in Osama's Jacuzzi.

In the *Parable of the Talents* (which we discussed earlier), the servant who was given the least amount of gold buried it. He considered his talent to be inferior to the other servants; *he stunted himself.* If we become regular, Comfortable Christians, we stunt our mission. When we lose sight of Christ's purpose, *we lose sight of ours.* Instead of attacking demonic strongholds, we find ourselves lured in while on assignment.

Where are Christ's good and faithful servants? We're calling in sick, absent without leave, or back in orientation.

PROCESSED CHRISTIANITY

"Then Jesus declared, 'I am the bread of life. He who comes to me will never go hungry.'" John 6:35

Bread is the foundation of a proper diet. But there are all kinds: French bread, sourdough bread, cornbread – the list goes on. Do all breads lead to nutrition? To answer that question, you must examine whether your bread is made with whole grains or enriched flour.

Contrary to its name, enriched flour will not enrich your health. It's called *enriched* because nutrients have been added to overcompensate for naturally occurring ones that are lost in processing. That's why we have loaves that advertise, "more calcium than milk!" These added nutrients are often of neither original quality nor usefulness. Liken it to being robbed of 10,000 dollars and reimbursed with 20,000 pesos. *You're enriched!*

Some of these added nutrients may actually be harmful. They may even lead to various health issues. *You're enriched!*

"They exchanged the truth about God for a lie, and worshipped and served created things rather than the Creator – who is forever praised. Amen." Romans 1:25

Material lust has robbed our wholeness. Instead of love, we take sex. Instead of joy, we settle for happiness. Instead of truth, we accept comforting lies. We're not even interested in seeking truth, because much like enriched bread, our path tastes better.

People have enriched the truth to appeal. The very essence that brought wholeness has been lost in the processing of mainstream Christianity. It has lost nutrient value and has proven to be harmful. When we serve an enriched Jesus, we become enriched adherents. And just as enriched properties can produce health problems, our enriched faith produces spiritual ones.

"Therefore go and make disciples of all nations, baptizing them in the name of the Father and the Son and the Holy Spirit." Matthew 28:19

Two thousand years ago, a handful of disciples were given the command to spread the Gospel, the *whole* Gospel. Today, practically everyone has heard some *variation* of it; we're two billion strong. But our enriched gospel has lost its quality and overcompensated with quantity.

QUANTITY OVER QUALITY

Consider the food packing industry. It's lowered quality to produce more affordable, cheaper meat. This enables fast food restaurants to serve us ninety-nine cent tacos. However, there are some unsavory techniques in processing these foods: genetic modification, synthetic additives, and mechanical recovery.

First, genetic modification changes the actual DNA of plants and animals to increase their yield. Second, synthetic additives are used to increase shelf life and sweeten products. Last but not least, mechanically recovered meats are a combination of animal scraps and cartilage that would otherwise be discarded, but instead have been minced and deliciously flavored. *Yum!*

We know processed food is junk, but it compensates by being cheap, convenient, and fast. But who can take it seriously?

For centuries, Western culture has processed Christianity by making faith a synonym of custom. Our numbers peaked as the cost of professing Christ plummeted. We have: 1) modified the makeup of a disciple (*it no longer requires discipline*) 2) sweetened difficult teachings and polarizing beliefs, and 3) recovered scraps of Christian consciousness. Who can take this faith seriously?

AN IMPRACTICAL COST

At a considerably higher cost, there are organic options that follow strict guidelines to keep purity and quality in food. You can buy cage-free, no hormone meats, and organically grown fruits and vegetables. But the price — similar to following Jesus's blueprint — may seem impractical.

"Then Jesus said to his disciples, 'Whoever wants to be my disciple must deny themselves and take up their cross and follow me.'" Matthew 16:24

Jesus attracted the masses with teachings and miracles. However, He was incredibly picky with who He allowed to actually follow Him. There are several examples of people who were willing to give up almost everything. *Almost.*

A teacher of the law asked Jesus if he could follow Him. He rebutted, saying, "Foxes have dens and birds have nests, but the Son of man has no place to lay his head" (Matthew 8:20). As if to say, "Are you sure you want to do this?" On another occasion, a rich man came to Jesus. He credentialed himself by claiming to have followed all of the commandments. Jesus told him to first sell all of his possessions and then come to Him. Sadly, he turned away.

Even the disciples were puzzled, wondering who could be saved. It's as if Jesus wants us to give up everything that matters to us: our lives, our possessions, our *comfort.* Like many other Christians, we find this prerequisite to be impractical, so we follow from afar.

CROSS-EXAMINATION

"To the Jews who had believed him, Jesus said, 'If you hold to my teaching, you are really my disciples.'" John 8:31

Have you ever acknowledged your faith to someone, and they were surprised because there was no prior indication? *It's embarrassing.* What if they thought you were joking, "Ha-ha, stop playing man." "*No, for real!*"

Imagine being on trial for your faith in a country where Christianity is illegal, and the judge acquits you based on a lack of evidence. Your friends and co-workers are cross-examined, all corroborating that, just ten minutes ago, you were gossiping, cursing, or rambling about sexual conquests.

Jesus warned us to recognize false believers. But before we point out the speck in our neighbor's eye, let us check the log in our own (Matthew 7:3). Are we holding onto His teachings, or do we *only believe* that Jesus is God?

A MODEST PROPOSAL TO PREVENT CHURCH CLOSURES:
A satirical letter

As a Christian, it pains me to witness the plight of the modern church. Across our nation, churches are closing their doors — *permanently*. Attendance is dwindling due to a) the lack of youth retention, coupled with b) the inevitable mortality of the aging majority. Simply put, *congregations are shrinking with every funeral!* Once-brimming churches have been reduced to humble gatherings of senior citizens singing "Kumbaya, my Lord" as they sit Indian style — if their achy joints permit.

Although this fate has been foreseen, we the church, have been unable to halt the downward spiral. And the more time passes, it becomes harder for the aging church to connect with the youth. *Sure, we've tried.* Many churches have employed *cool* youth pastors. Some of these youth pastors are even adorned with tattoos — a once damnable curse kin to the mark on Cain's face after killing his brother, Abel.

Another step we've taken to circumvent the virtual bleeding away of our youth is to remix our classic hymnals. Sadly, the incorporation of loud and undecipherable music has done little to retain their attention. We've placed a band-aid on a severed limb.

This downward spiral has led to yet another problem – bills. Bills, combined with inflation, building maintenance, and attendance reduction, have driven up the cost, per capita, of keeping our doors open. The cost of running a church becomes a proverbial 'cross to bear' — not just the cross, but the brick and mortar on which it stands. Simply put, *we're strapped for cash!*

Some churches have remedied this by increasing tithes — shaking down the remaining faithful. Others, if they have existed long enough, are able to use their historical value as a museum or a venue for movie shoots — a phenomenon often seen in big cities like Los Angeles. But this source of income only helps to offset the costs of a small fraction of churches. What about a church in the middle of *God knows where?* They should to turn to alternative sources of revenue – for example, leasing.

Sure, some have rented out space to smaller church groups, but why stop there?

If there's one asset a church still retains, it's real estate. And as the cost of property rises, so does a church's value — *at least monetarily.* Silver lining? *No!* It's *gold...* frankincense, and myrrh! Christianity may be dying in the West, but it's left us a *hell* of an inheritance!

A church building only operates certain hours, rendering a perfectly good property unused for the majority of the week. Imagine the funds that could be raked in – *for God's kingdom* – if a building was rented out commercially. It would put less strain on its members, many of whom are surviving on pension and social security checks (the old, the ignorant, and the old and ignorant!).

So what kind of businesses would we lease to? To ensure less turnover, churches should only accept applications from lucrative, in-demand businesses –perhaps businesses that their own congregations would also subscribe to.

I beg you to weigh out what I am about to propose, as it may at first seem objectionable. In my opinion, the ideal lessee would be a buffet restaurant, a sports bar, or nightclub. *A bit crass?* I initially objected as well.

I hate to see church buildings being sold to other dealings. The first thing they do is take down our blessed cross. I shook my head once as I drove by a gorgeous cathedral that had been converted into an insurance office! *–a den of robbers!* As I began fashioning a whip and clearing my throat to yell, *"It is written: My house will be called a house of prayer!"* it dawned on me. Why was I so concerned about the plight of a building once dedicated to God, now being used for other purposes *if* I've overlooked how I, the *real temple of God*, have no qualms operating for both Christ and flesh?

How fitting would it be then, if my church building housed opposing establishments as well – establishments that serve both the purposes of God and material desire.

Leasing church property to a buffet restaurant (gluttony), a sports bar (idolatry and substance abuse), or a nightclub (revelry and lust) would only mimic the ways in which we, the real temples of God, operate in our off hours. Instead of taking down that blessed cross, we keep it up ... *while simultaneously opposing it.*

There is nothing holy about a brick and mortar construction. The holy vessel is the body, which we constantly defile. So if we can overlook this greater contradiction, then why nitpick at a surface level discrepancy: the conflicting usage of a building? Why fight for the sanctity of the sanctuary – *it's only symbolic.*

"Don't you know that you yourselves are God's temple and that God's Spirit dwells in your midst?" 1 Corinthians 3:16

PART 5:
THE DANGER

SCREENED BY SCREENS

We wake up to the alarm on our cell phone. If we're not running late, we may flip through some social media apps. If we *are* running late, we may flip through some social media apps. On our way to school or work, on our breaks, or any possible downtime – a red light or an elevator ride – we're glued to our screens.

At our fingertips we have access to social media, e-mail, texting, games, and the Internet. We also have a Bible app, *but it's not Sunday*. We get home and flip on the television screen. At the same time, we may again check our cell phone screen, and/or the laptop screen. Maybe we'll catch a movie tonight, *"oooo"* a bigger screen! Lastly, we go to sleep and set the alarm on our cell phone screen. We've come full circle, screened by screens.

PICKED OFF

One of the most fundamental strategies in basketball is the pick-n-roll. The player with the ball waits for his teammate to 'set the screen,' and then he runs behind him – stifling a chasing defender. Depending on a defender's awareness of the trap, he either recovers *or* falls on his back. The latter effectively creates a breakdown in the team's defense.

Sometimes the defender falls for the same screen over and over, oftentimes pleading to the referee to bail him out. Ultimately, he fails to achieve his purpose. He was called to defend.

BE KEEN OF YOUR SCREEN

The purpose of a screen is to distract us from our purpose; *it's purpose is fulfilled when our purpose is not.* It makes us lose focus. Depending on our awareness, we either change our tactics or get distracted again. Sometimes we fall for the same screen, over and over.

The devil is constantly looking to screen every moment that we seek God. Taking away our purpose fulfills his purpose. We're convinced that we don't have time; but really, we don't make time. We haven't made the proper adjustments in anticipation of the distractions. Ultimately, we fail to achieve our purpose – being Christ-like.

FACTOR THE DISTRACTER

As much as we hate distracted drivers, many of us still text and drive. We look up, we look down; we swerve right, we swerve left. Not only have we increased the risk of crashing, but more importantly (depending on perspective), the risk of making egregious spelling errors. The recipient is left confused, trying to decipher the message. What the heck did we just send?

The problem with being distracted is that we mess up on both accounts, driving and texting. Depending on which purpose is more important, the other action is a distraction. The messaging is the distraction if it's more important to drive safely. But if it's more important to send messages, then the driving is the distraction.

We're in constant conflict of what our purpose is. We want to satisfy both worldly and spiritual urges simultaneously, but we can't do either right. So let's factor the distracter by identifying which purpose is more important. Maybe God is distracting us from enjoying what this world has to offer. Or maybe this world is distracting us from what God has to offer. We should pursue whichever purpose we find to be more important. If we try to do both, we'll fail at both.

FACETIME WITH GOD

"My heart says of you, 'Seek his face!' Your face, Lord, I will seek."
Psalm 27:8

Why do we send text messages anyway? Well, texting cuts to the point. We like quick conversations. Sometimes, the last thing we want when we ask, "How are you doing?" is for someone to tell us! We often text a random question to someone, even if we haven't spoken to them in months – without inquiring about their livelihood. Texting keeps it short and sweet.

On the other hand, if we wanted to be personal, we may schedule a video chat so we can be face to face. Unlike phone calls or text messages that do not require our undivided attention, FaceTime is often planned or done when we have no other distractions.

When we're too distracted to devote time to God, we try to send Him little messages. We don't realize how confused our prayers are. How is He supposed to respond to our gibberish? We need to devote a time when all distractions are eliminated, a time to seek His face, a time when we perhaps close our eyes and meditate – which should *only* be done while driving if we're 'seeking His face' in the *literal* sense.

THE BIG THREE

"For everything in the world – the lust of the flesh, the lust of the eyes, and the pride of life – comes not from the Father but from the world. The world and its desires pass away, but whoever does the will of God lives forever." 1 John 2:16

Worldliness – it's a term Christians often use to describe *external* behavior. It usually refers to where we hangout, who we hang out with, and what activities we do when we're hangin' out. But worldliness is *internal*, because it begins with our heart.

There are three main attitudes that encompass worldliness:
1) **The lust of the flesh**. This is characterized by a preoccupation with gratifying physical desires.
2) **The lust of the eyes**. This is characterized by materialism, craving the accumulation of things.
3) **Boasting and pride**. This is characterized by an obsession with personal status and importance, *or the lack thereof.* It can also manifest as self-pity.

The main screens of seeking God are our desires pertaining to physical gratification, possessions, and pride. They're the treasures of this world; they make us lose focus, *over and over.*

Jesus faced these three temptations in the wilderness when He was fasting. He was tempted to turn a stone into bread (lust of the flesh), worship Satan to gain an earthly kingdom (lust of the eyes), and jump off of a cliff (pride). The latter temptation appealed to His personal importance – Satan claimed that angels would save Him.

INDULGING IN THE SPIRIT

If God would just speak to us, we would know exactly what to do. The Bible tells us of people whom He directly instructed. Did they see a light, a vision?

We've often heard people say that God told them something, or that He "put this on my heart." Some claim to have been given a 'word of knowledge.' *Anyone can say that.* In fact, Jesus warned us that many people would. We must hear from God ourselves – *noting that His sheep know His voice* (John 10:27).

"While they were worshiping the Lord and fasting, the Holy Spirit said, 'Set apart for me Barnabas and Saul for the work to which I have called them.'" Acts 13:2

Worship and fasting set the table for the Holy Spirit to: speak, give us guidance, and set us apart. We often expect His direction without first clearing out our own thoughts and distractions. When we worship, we give worth to God above all of our physical desires. It's not a playlist on iTunes, or an emotional rush at conference, but rather, a lifestyle.

Fasting, on the other hand, is such an uncomfortable observance that we rarely do it. We can stomach a social media fast. After all, *we don't need it and it makes us less productive.* However, food is fundamental for survival. When we fast from food, we're expressing that seeking Christ is worth more than our physical needs.

Worship and fasting compliment each other. A worship lifestyle exemplifies that our indulgence is not our *physical desires.* A fasting lifestyle exemplifies that our indulgence is not in our *physical needs.* Our only indulgence is in Him.

"Meanwhile his disciples urged him, 'Rabbi, eat something.' But he said to them, 'I have food to eat that you know nothing about.'" John 4:31-32

Food isn't just a need; it's our greatest material desire. Would we rather eat an engineered cracker that contained all necessary nutrients, or a rib-eye steak? Consider the children of Israel who were sick of the bread that fell from heaven. *Food is pleasure,* and every day we look forward to our meals. We want something tasty – something that makes us salivate in anticipation, *much like Pavlov's dog.* We're excited when the holiday season comes so that we can indulge in turkey, ham, stuffing, pies, cookies, and drinks.

Fasting, prayer, and meditation draw us closer to God in a way that makes us realize we can't rely on our flesh. These disciplines prepare our hearts for God to speak, to guide us. The question is whether we're willing to give up what it takes to listen.

Many of us fail to practice Christianity as a form of asceticism. In fact, we may practice it as if the goal were to reach material prosperity! If so, our indulgence is not in God, but in materials. We seek first His kingdom, *hoping that ours will follow.* We give so that we can get.

Jesus told the crowds that they were only looking for Him because He gave them loaves and fish (John 6:26). He knew that their indulgence was not in His words, but in physical desire. Their hearts were not truly His. *Are ours?*

CARDIAC ARREST

Consider why Jesus turned away the rich man who wanted to follow Him. The man valued his wealth *more than* following Christ. His heart was given to material indulgence – he worshiped money more than he worshiped God. The ascetic nature of following Christ was too much for him. *Is it too much for us?*

"Create in me a pure heart, O God, and renew a steadfast spirit within me." Psalm 51:10

The only way to cleanse oneself of worldly desires is a change of heart. Zacchaeus was also a rich man, but he was so humbled that Jesus would come to his house that he gave half of his money to the poor and repaid all whom he had cheated four times. His heart's desire was arrested by a new purpose; *everything else was just a distraction.*

BATH WITH BATHSEBA

"One thing I ask of the Lord, this is what I seek: that I may dwell in the house of the Lord all the days of my life, to gaze upon the beauty of the Lord and to seek him in his temple." Psalm 27:4

King David was known to be a man after God's own heart. His greatest desire was to live in God's presence, but he too had his share of distractions. While his army was away at war, he saw one of his soldier's wives, Bathsheba, bathing (What a fitting name).

Distracted by lust, he compromised and slept with her, and she became pregnant. Frantically, he called her husband to return, hoping he'd sleep with his wife to conceal his sin. But the husband was focused on his purpose, which was to fight for Israel. So David obliged him. In fact, he had him placed on the front lines... to die.

We must be aware of the screens. The enemy uses them to make us lose sight of our purpose. If we allow ourselves to be distracted by pride, the lust of our flesh and eyes, then we prevent God from guiding our lives.

THE PITY PARTY

"Yet when I surveyed all that my hands had done and what I had toiled to achieve, everything was meaningless, a chasing after the wind; nothing was gained under the sun." Ecclesiastes 2:11

To the world, the definition of success is being able to indulge *in the three screens:* material wealth, sex, and status. Let's say there's this guy, 'Mr. Richie,' who chose a high-paying career for the purpose of fulfilling all three. 'Mr. Poore,' on the other hand, chose a career that doesn't pay well, but is inwardly purposeful. If they pull alongside each other during traffic — Mr. Richie in his *Mercedes Benz* and Mr. Poore in a sputtering *Nissan Minimum* — who is to be pitied?

If Mr. Poore becomes envious of Mr. Richie, Poore has lost purpose; *he's been screened.* Mr. Richie can't help him re-store focus. After all, when he glances at Mr. Poore's miserable car and miserable expression, it reinforces his own material, sensual, and prideful purpose.

"If only for this life we have hope in Christ, we are of all people most to be pitied." 1 Corinthians 15:19

So many of us have lost the purpose in serving Christ. We're seemingly hampered by commandments, salivating as the world indulges in earthly lust. As we compare our lives with our friends, classmates, and co-workers, it seems like they're enjoying life.

Our faith becomes both restrictive and unrewarding. The more we stare at them, the more we lose focus. In addition, our inner confliction reinforces their purpose.

ONLY GOD CAN JUDGE ME

People who have come under public scrutiny often thwart liability with the ironclad defense: "Only God can judge me". The late rapper Tupac popularized this phrase – and he may have finally been granted his appeal. The concept behind the argument is: I am not obligated to answer to you.

Jesus pointed out that people who judge are often guilty of the same sin, if not worse. *Hypocrites!* God is the ultimate judge, so it shouldn't matter what other sinners think about you, right?

"So I strive always to keep my conscience clear before God and man." Acts 24:16

The Apostle Paul was constantly subjected to accusations from hypocritical Jews, pagans, and even Christians. He expressed his effort to be blameless, not only before God, but man as well. But why did he feel obligated to them?

"Then Agrippa said to Paul, 'Do you think that in such a short time you can persuade me to be a Christian?'" Acts 26:28

Even after being incarcerated for years, he addressed false and exaggerated accusations with love, using his trial as an opportunity to witness. Once again, we may not be able to *easily persuade* people to become Christians, but we may *easily persuade* them not to be. Our reaction to being judged, regardless of our innocence or even the hypocrisy of our accusers, can turn people off to Christ.

By lashing back, we may be witnessing against Christ instead of witnessing for Him. We gain nothing by throwing stones back. Is the church full of hypocrites? Sure. Is the world full of hypocrites? Sure. But let's not use that as an opportunity to relinquish our obligation to both God and man (Romans 1:14).

THE VERDICT

How is it that we find solace in appealing to the judgment of a holy, sin-hating Deity, instead of accepting a human verdict? Can anything be more daunting than answering to the Father, Son, and Holy Spirit – a jury of our superiors?

What makes the 'Only God can judge me' motion so appealing is that it defers judgment for an indefinite amount of time. *It's a form of procrastination.* Essentially, we're putting judgment out of the foreseeable future with the hope that it doesn't even exist. *Brilliant!* After all, no one wants to be judged, right?

The concept of being judged has a negative connotation. But consider this: a workplace performance review isn't a bad thing if we've been good and faithful servants. In fact, we may even look forward to this form of judgment, as it may bring forth a reward. Depending on our religion, that reward may be seven smoking hot virgins! *(Sorry, Christians).*

It's understandable why nonbelievers are uneasy about the idea of God's judgment, but why do Christians suppress the idea? This is our opportunity to witness about how the cross clears our sin! We're the 'righteousness of Christ,' *right?*

The problem is, we haven't been the best Christians.

DON'T KILL MY VIBE

Our faith in Jesus doesn't necessarily result in a victorious walk. We can all relate to Kendrick Lamar's lyric, "I am a sinner, who's probably gonna sin again, Lord forgive me." But have you ever considered the odds of being in the middle of a future sin during the Christ's Second Coming? *God-forbid!*

There are 3 main factors to take into consideration:
a= degree of sin committed (white lie to murder)
b= rate of sins committed (sins per minute)
c= chance of a Second Coming even happening (unknown – think of it as 'x' in algebra)

Ideally, Jesus will arrive in our sleep – since being unconscious greatly diminishes our ability to sin (Although the *unconscious defense* may be void if we're bedside a lover). The only way we could be cleared then, is if we prayed for forgiveness right after we finished! Hopefully our lover prays too; we'd hate to be raptured without 'em. There's a small window before fading into sleep that we can use to whisper, "Lord forgive me."

Eventually, we see beyond our own bull-crap; we stop praying for God's grace. Instead of falling to *a* sin, we begin living *in* sin. But we're still Christians, *right?* We just don't want Jesus to return (right now).

Instead of having the fear of the Lord, we become fearful of the Lord. Instead of eagerly awaiting His return like a true follower, our hope is that He doesn't return – well, for now. After all, He might not claim us.

"If we deliberately keep on sinning after we have received the knowledge of the truth, no sacrifice for sins is left, but only a fearful expectation of judgment and of raging fire that will consume the enemies of God." Hebrews 10:26-27

BEYOND UNREASONABLE DOUBT

According to our beliefs, the world will be held accountable on Judgment Day. Some may anticipate fire and brimstone befalling every homosexual and atheist — a double portion reserved for *homosexual atheists.* Won't we rise to our feet and give the Righteous Judge a standing ovation? *Finally,* justice has been served to the heathen!

As hypocritical Christians, our judgment may actually be worse than one doled out to non-believers (Romans 2:1-3). It would be better if we too had not known the path of righteousness (2 Peter 2:21). Therefore, we Comfortable Christians, actually have *more incentive* to believe that God doesn't exist. *Go figure!*

In the Western world, less and less people are affiliating themselves with Christianity. Those raised in the faith are jumping ship into a sea of agnosticism. Those who remain faithful share a similar struggle — wrestling with their doubt of God. But sometimes, doubt can be a bit unreasonable.

REFERENCE POINTS

Doubt prevents progression by questioning all the moments in our lives when we knew that our God, our faith, our salvation was real. *Was.* Doubt doesn't take into consideration the points in our lives when we couldn't deny God... *at least for that moment.* These are our reference points.

Consider the Israelites, God's chosen people who were delivered from Egypt. After generations of slavery, they witnessed miracles so great, many people don't believe the stories. But that's okay because shortly after, *neither did they.*

As the Israelites walked through the parted waters, they must have been in total awe. God must have been so real to them, *in that moment*. Reference point. But when they got to the other side, they began to murmur, saying that Moses had brought them to the wilderness to die. Some even wanted to go back to Egypt – perhaps hoping Moses would *re-part* the Red Sea.

Why would the same God that brought you out of slavery let you die in a desert? Surely the *miraculous exodus* should have been enough to convince them of His guidance. The Israelites witnessed many wonders, but their doubt was *miraculously unfazed!* They saw the plagues, the pillars of fire that blocked Pharaoh, the Red Sea parting, and manna coming from heaven. But no matter how great God's work was, their doubt *rose to the occasion!* And when they came to take Canaan, God wasn't great enough.

LORD OF THE GRASSHOPPERS

"We went into the land to which you sent us, and it does flow with milk and honey! Here is its fruit. But the people who live there are powerful, We can't attack those people; they are stronger than we are. We seemed like grasshoppers in our own eyes, and we looked the same to them." Numbers 13: 27-28, 31, 33

They were like grasshoppers, and they made God a grasshopper too. Albeit, *Lord of the Grasshoppers!* Their doubt prevented an entire generation from realizing the vision. Instead of entering the Promised Land, they wandered the desert for the rest of their lives.

We know that God has a vision for us; His Word tells us that He is faithful to complete the work He began (Philippians 1:6). But oftentimes, doubt creeps into our minds and begins to question our faith. It fixates our eyes on our current problem instead of our God. We quickly forget our reference points and never enter the Promised Land. If we're not fulfilling God's vision, then we're wandering a spiritual desert.

Ahh the desert: a barren and fruitless land. Many Comfortable Christians have camped out here. The rent is cheap, depending on one's relative value of purpose. The more we wander in doubt, the more likely we are to die there, never fulfilling the vision. We spend our time pondering whether God has a plan for us, or if He's even real.

Ultimately, doubt leads to the loss of vision, which leads to fruitlessness.

THE PROBLEM OF EVIL

"See to it that no one takes you captive through hollow and deceptive philosophy, which depends on human tradition." Colossians 2:8

We must be prepared to confront doubt by knowing the Word better than the enemy. After all, the devil used God's word to introduce doubt in Eve's heart. One of the most common questions is: If God is good, then why does He allow so much evil to exist in the world? *What is evil,* really?

To God, lying, idolatry, fornication – even thinking about fornication – is evil. In fact, if you're guilty of breaking one commandment, you've broken all (James 2:10). So are we asking God to destroy us too? But wait: hold your hellfire! We're only talking about the evil things that we – the evil people – think should be punished.

For example, everyone in prison has been found guilty of a crime. But some crimes are even hated by criminals. Inmates have been known to beat and kill child molesters. Even criminals have standards, skewed as they may be.

Should we fire the judge and let the criminals judge themselves, a true jury of *their* peers? They can base their verdicts on their relative morals, judge on a curve, and not absolute law. Sure, only a few criminals would ever be convicted, *but* we'd save millions of tax dollars in prison costs! Those dollars can then be used for subsequently needed state-of-the-art home security, personal bodyguards, and bulletproof vests.

You see, we want God to be inconsistent like us, picking and choosing what evil gets eliminated. We justify ourselves by looking at our neighbors, who are also sinful. We've categorized our evil deeds. After all, murder is not the same thing as lying, according to *our* understanding.

LEAN ON YOUR OWN MISUNDERSTANDING

"Trust in the Lord with all your heart and lean not on your own understanding; in all your ways submit to him, and he will make your paths straight." Proverbs 3:5-6

Many people struggle with believing in Jesus, others with believing in the Creator. After all, God isn't visible. Why can't He just show us that He's real, once and for all? Why won't God just do something so we can all believe?

What do we want, *some miracle?* Some sign to show us that He exists, like He did for the Israelites? Maybe God can part the freeway at rush hour. Let's demand a sign from heaven! The Pharisees also demanded a sign from Jesus... aside from all of the *miraculous healings*. If Jesus is real, why doesn't He just prove Himself so we can believe? Maybe He could be a guest speaker this Sunday – do a couple miracles and feed us fish and chips.

"A wicked and adulterous generation looks for a sign." Matthew 16:4

As much as we think a miracle upon our request would give us unfailing faith, it won't. The Israelites are a measure of ourselves. And if they could witness the grandest of miracles in the Bible and still doubt, so will we.

I met a girl who told me she prayed to God even though she didn't believe He existed. She promised Jesus that she would return to church if He somehow got rid of her $1,000 traffic fine. *Desperate times call for desperate measures.*

The officer who cited her didn't show up on the court date; *she was free to go!* But she's still an atheist. It was *obviously* a coincidence, she reasoned. After all, she wasn't the only one who got off; there's too much room for doubt.

Sometimes we think God is inconsistent, when really, it's us who are variable.

One of the many miracles Jesus performed was casting out demons. I was raised in an atmosphere where this type of deliverance ministry was commonplace. Many people excuse the behaviors of the possessed as a mental problem, while others think it's only in movies. But I consistently witnessed spirits responding to, and being driven out by the power of Jesus's name.

There's a moment that sticks out to me even more. My father was preaching in Africa when the Holy Spirit warned him about an evil force that was coming from the right side of the audience. He told the church, and everyone begin rebuking the devil in that direction. Then a great commotion ensued as an extremist Muslim was caught with a grenade and a sword. He had come to kill my father.

God's power was undeniable to me, *in those moments.*

ORDER IN THE COURT

Our legal system has a term known as reasonable doubt. Before coming to a verdict, the prosecution must provide proof beyond a reasonable doubt —assuming the jurors to be reasonable people. This procedure is in place to prevent the innocent from being wrongly convicted. But how does one validate the reasonability of doubt?

Witnesses may doubt what they have seen – even fail to recall it accurately. Their credibility itself can be doubted! Before jurors come to a consensus, they mull over their uncertainties, often swayed by the convictions of other jurors, not their own. Ultimately, our court system condemns many who are innocent, and acquits many who are guilty.

Unless we have a vested interest in the case, we just shrug our shoulders and hope that karma somehow catches up to criminals. (Maybe on the repeat offense). The system isn't perfect, but it's the best we have. What does that mean? Our best judgment still fails us.

If the reasonability of doubt can come into question in our highest courts, picture how much less use it has in a kingdom based on faith. If doubt can wreak havoc on the physical—on facts and things we once thought were black and white—how much more havoc can doubt cause in our trust of things we can't see? Skepticism comes naturally and is intensified in the supernatural.

AMAZING FAITH

Jesus once healed a blind man after asking him if he believed, and *his faith made him whole.* On another occasion, a centurion asked for the healing of his servant. When Jesus asked whether He should come to his home, the centurion said, "'Lord, I do not deserve to have you come under my roof. Just say the word, and my servant will be healed'" (Matthew 8:8). Amazed, Jesus pronounced it the greatest faith in Israel and healed his servant instantly.

What would it take to amaze God by our faith? It's more likely that we're amazing Him with our lack of it. Even the disciples struggled to believe after witnessing Him walk on water, heal the sick, and even resurrect the dead. They asked, "Lord, show us the Father and that will be enough for us." Was it an unreasonable request? (*Doubt is truly incredible*). He responded, "How can you say, 'Show us the Father'? Don't you believe I am in the Father, and that the Father is in me?" (John 14:8-10).

Jesus brought many evidences that were beyond reasonable doubt. But no amount of evidence can satisfy *unreasonable* doubt.

"Then Jesus told him, 'Because you have seen me, you have believed; blessed are those who have not seen and yet have believed.'" John 20:29

Doubting Thomas (as he will be eternally known), refused to believe the report that Jesus had resurrected. It wasn't until he saw with his own eyes and touched the holes in His hands that he believed. If a disciple had trouble believing, then it's understandable that we doubt too.

Even when Jesus was alive in the flesh, teaching and healing, the witnesses in His hometown doubted. "Where did this man get this wisdom and miraculous powers? Isn't this the carpenter's son?" (Matthew 13:54-55). Because of their lack of faith, He left without doing many miracles. Likewise, we limit His ability to work in our lives when we doubt Him.

JUDGING JESUS

"'The reason I was born and came into the world is to testify to the truth. Everyone on the side of truth listens to me.' 'What is truth?' retorted Pilate.'" John 18:38

Governor Pilate knew that the accusations brought against Jesus were unreasonable. But Jesus wouldn't defend Himself. When Christ explained His purpose was "to testify the truth," Pilate retorted, "What is truth?" He wasn't interested in learning what 'truth' was from a homeless preacher.

Today, many have the same retort: "What is truth?" It's not that we're interested in finding out, but that we consider truth to be vague and relative. Can we really find it in a homeless preacher who lived 2,000 years ago? Just as Pilate washed his hands as a symbol of relinquishing his responsibility of Jesus, many consider themselves free of responsibility, regarding what they've done with the knowledge of Him.

Is there *anything* more unreasonable than neglecting to seek potential truth? Perhaps we will eventually, when there's a sense of urgency. After all, desperate times call for desperate measures.

"But the new rebel is a skeptic, and will not entirely trust anything. He has no loyalty; therefore he can never be really a revolutionist. And the fact that he doubts everything really gets in his way when he wants to denounce anything. For all denunciation implies a moral doctrine of some kind; and the modern revolutionist doubts not only the institution he denounces, but the doctrine by which he denounces it. . . . As a politician, he will cry out that war is a waste of life, and then, as a philosopher, that all life is waste of time. A Russian pessimist will denounce a policeman for killing a peasant, and then prove by the highest philosophical principles that the peasant ought to have killed himself. . . . The man of this school goes first to a political meeting, where he complains that savages are treated as if they were beasts; then he takes his hat and umbrella and goes on to a scientific meeting, where he proves that they practically are beasts. In short, the modern revolutionist, being an infinite skeptic, is always engaged in undermining his own mines. In his book on politics he attacks men for trampling on morality; in his book on ethics he attacks morality for trampling on men. Therefore the modern man in revolt has become practically useless for all purposes of revolt. By rebelling against everything he has lost his right to rebel against anything." —G.K. Chesterton

SAY YO' PRAYERS, SUCKA!

We're all familiar with the cliché cartoon scene in which a character facing death says a turbo prayer. Whether a train is swiftly approaching or he's falling off of a cliff, his alarm drives him to make things right with God. Even in movies, a gunman may graciously advise his victim to, "Say yo' prayers, sucka!" However, the time allotted to pray is very brief.

What makes us chuckle is how relatable it is. When we're faced with death, we turn to God. Hopefully He will either save us or forgive our sinful lives. We're covering our bases, just in case He exists.

Let's consider how quickly death can arrive. If you've ever been in an accident, you've noticed how quickly things can spin out of control. There are so many ways to die, many of which fail to grant sufficient time to *say yo' prayers, sucka!*

 **Tip** Prepare for emergency repentance! Commit a short prayer to memory and practice saying it very fast.

Even if we manage to fire off a final prayer in Clint Eastwood-esque fashion, how much weight would it have? "Lord forgive me" is not a magic bullet; it isn't an earnest cry to change our lives, especially if we've waited until there isn't any life left.

There's a misconception that we can live our whole lives *willfully* sinning, but with our last breath rededicate ourselves to Christ. Are we either praying to a sucker – albeit, a divine sucker – or we are suckers for praying? Perhaps His goodness and mercy is so great that it goes beyond the bounds of suckership.

"Someone might argue, 'If my falsehood enhances God's truthfulness and so increases his glory, why am I still condemned as a sinner?'" Romans 3:7

In *The Parable of the Workers in the Vineyard*, Jesus told a story of a landowner who hired a bunch of unemployed, unskilled, and unwanted day laborers to work his vineyard. The landowner kept hiring more and more workers throughout the day, up until the final hour. He then paid each worker, *regardless of start time*, a denarius. Although this amount was far greater than any of them could expect, the workers who came in earliest grumbled that their pay was equal to those who came in at the final hour.

The parable was an analogy regarding God's system of grace – a system we often try to beat. We see a benefit in being the last of the workers who still received a denarius. For this reason, we postpone reconciling our lives with God until later – even up until the final hour. Hopefully we'll be able stave off judgment.

"For God did not send the Son into the world to judge the world, but that the world might be saved through him." John 3:17

Occasionally, someone will hold a door open for us to walk through. *It's a nice gesture.* Pleasantly surprised, we express gratitude with a smile; both parties are momentarily charmed. But sometimes, the person who holds the door does so although we're further off. *This is awkward.* Should the person holding the door realize the situation is uncomfortable and walk away, or should we do a brisk jog and weird smile? *"Heh*, yeah… thanks."

We'd rather open the door ourselves than to be pressured to move quickly, unless of course, it was closing time. If the store was being locked, but the manager was graciously holding the door, we'd be happier about being hurried.

"Moreover, no one knows when their hour will come: As fish are caught in a cruel net, or birds are taken in a snare, so people are trapped by evil times that fall unexpectedly upon them." Ecclesiastes 9:12

Although no man knows the day or hour of the Lord, every generation is certain that the apocalypse is near. But the importance of the end of the world pales in comparison to the end of *your* world. During the Cold War, Americans and Soviets were deadlocked in fear that nuclear war would break out and decimate the planet. But one could have just as easily been choked to death by a morsel of incredibly dry chicken breast. Tomorrow isn't promised, and the door that God is holding open for us may close. We should be thankful, not irritated, that we have an uncomfortable moment to scurry to Him.

NEGLECTED BY THE NEGLECTED

In *The Parable of the Great Banquet*, a man prepared a feast and invited many guests. He sent an invitation, saying, "Come, for everything is now ready" (Luke 14:17). But all of the guests were preoccupied – with their land, their possessions, or their relationships. So instead, he invited the poor, the lame, the blind. We often claim to depend on Jesus, but we may really depend on possessions and relationships. And our preoccupation with these things may cause us to ultimately neglect Christ.

"Come to me, all you who are weary and burdened, and I will give you rest." Matthew 11:28

As a society, we try to accommodate to handicapped people. But many of our structures still fail them. I once came across a wheelchair-bound man as he struggled to go up an incline. He kept rolling back into a busy street! I ran to his aid saying, "Sir, can I give you a hand?" He looked at me with disgust, and replied, "I don't need your help!" *I was baffled!* He didn't want sympathy; he had faith in himself. But what he failed to see was that I wasn't thinking about his handicap. I was thinking about his life.

Imagine someone trapped in an inferno in a building several stories high. Smoke and fire are making it hard to breathe as he collapses. *He's virtually handicapped.* Gloriously, a firefighter arrives, but he doesn't need his sympathy! He can make it on his own. He retorts, "Don't be fooled just because I'm face-down in a burning building with a structure that may be compromised at any moment; *I have a plan!*"

This is similar to the way we rebuff Jesus.

"For God so loved the world that he gave his one and only Son, that whoever believes in him shall not perish but have eternal life." John 3:16

The very structures in which we put our faith – wealth, health, and relationships – may collapse on us. These are the very things that preoccupy us from accepting Christ's invitation. And we're perishing with them. Instead of allowing Jesus to guide us through, we seek our own way. Sometimes we try to get our lives right first, failing to realize that Jesus isn't thinking about our sins; His concern is with our eternal lives.

Many of us have accepted His invitation, but we're focused on something valuable we left in a burning structure: *this material world.* Somehow it's worth risking everything to go back inside.

In search of more to rescue, the Good Shepherd finds us again, in the same burning room. "I thought I already saved you?" Instead of compelling others to join His banquet, we're in a cycle of rededicating our lives. One day, the structure we keep running back inside of may collapse upon us, leaving us little time to say our prayers.

IDENTITY THEFT

If you're on the run from the law, just call a guy who knows a guy, who will forge you a new identity, a new passport, and even a new line of credit… or *so I've seen in movies.* You then flee the country, leaving behind your old crimes, your old home, and sadly your old friends and family. But as you cross international waters, you think, "Behold! I am a new creation, old things have passed away!" (2 Corinthian 5:17). The only way the law can catch you now is if you come back, perhaps suckered by nostalgia.

The only escape from the penalty of sin is a new identity, a new citizenship, and Christ's line of credit — *His righteousness.* But all this could be undone if we succumb to a nostalgic mindset of the former life. There, the *accuser of the brethren* lies in wait, in stakeout-esque fashion. As you return to your old life, he smirks, "Behold! He is an old creation, new things have passed away!" The devil wants nothing more than to rob us of our new identity in Christ.

"God made him who had no sin to be sin for us, so that in him we might become the righteousness of God." 2 Corinthians 5:21

VICTIM #1

Identity theft is the fastest growing crime in America. Culprits have become very crafty. Some use *phishing schemes* to trick people into giving up sensitive information. For example, Victim #1 happily forks over his bank account information, expecting to receive a deposit from an entity that somehow owes him money — perhaps a *Nigerian prince!*

Another scheme targets classified ads. Thieves pay for something with a check that is valued *higher* than the cost of the sale. The thief asks the seller to send the change. For instance,

Victim #1 deposits the check and his account looks great! Gleefully, he sends the change. But days later, the check comes up void. Victim #1 thought he could trust the thief because the thief trusted him first, albeit with a fake check.

Other thieves create websites that look like the ones we intended to reach. But a closer look at the address bar shows that something is off. Once again, Victim #1 doesn't realize this until there has been considerable damage. *It's been a bad week for Victim #1.*

UNSEEN ENEMIES

How easy would it be for identity thieves to rob us if we didn't believe they existed, or doubted that we'd be attacked? Although we haven't seen them, we see the charges they make. So if we value our identity — the key to our credit and resources — then we'll be on guard.

Rarely does one react in a calm, collected manner upon the realization that his/her wallet or purse is stolen. Our identity is everything. If we can't prove who we are, we can't buy anything! Meanwhile, someone may be proving they are us and are buying *everything.*

Without our identity, we feel lost. If it doesn't turn up immediately, we'll call the bank, cancel the old card, and request a new one. Hopefully, no one has used our identity.

The book *The Screwtape Letters* satirically portrays human life through the eyes of Screwtape, a well seasoned, senior-level devil. He sends mentoring letters to his nephew, Wormwood, who has just begun his demonic career in the service of "Our Father Below." The book provokes people to question their philosophical presumptions. We may not physically see the dark forces, but we may see how they manipulate us.

"The thief comes only to steal and kill and destroy; I have come that they may have life, and have it to the full." John 10:10

The devil's existence is evidenced by his work: stealing, killing, and destroying. But believing he exists is not enough. He can still rob us if we're not guarding our identity in Christ. He *phishes* for our attention, hoping to fool us into thinking that we will gain something if we just give up our identity. He offers a life that we think has value, but that we later find to be void. *But the most vicious scam is imitation.* Subscribing to Comfortable Christianity leads us to believe that our faith is in good standing with God. Under closer examination, we may realize that to be far from true.

We must be vigilant in securing our identity in Jesus. If we ever lose sight of it, our focus should be immediately finding it, like the search for a lost wallet. The devil is always looking for ways to rob us. Without the full armor of God, we leave ourselves vulnerable to his schemes (Ephesians 6:11).

ZERO LIABILITY

"What shall we say, then? Shall we go on sinning so that grace may increase?" Romans 6:1

Even if someone steals our identity, we can call our bank and they will credit us. This has become both a gift and a curse. It often fosters an attitude of *zero liability,* ultimately hurting the fight against the thieves. People seem to think it's okay to have their identity stolen as long as they're reimbursed.

What if we realized our identity was stolen but figured we'd call the bank later. After all, it's happened before, no biggie. Days or weeks pass and then we finally call. The bank will want to know why we took so long to report it. Now *we* have become a liability.

If we take a zero liability attitude to our protecting our identity in Christ —thinking we will ultimately be forgiven — we allow the devil to win. Our Comfortable Christian lifestyles tarnish Christ's reputation in the eyes of a skeptical world. Now *we* have become a liability.

If we're not operating in Christ's identity, then our faith in God can only condemn us. The Word says that deliberately sinning makes us the *enemies of God* who trample on Jesus (Hebrews 10:29).

ALLOW ME TO EXPLAIN

Few moments are more embarrassing than having our credit card declined. We've all been there. Either, a) at a register with groceries bagged and people waiting behind, or b) at a restaurant and the waiter gently whispers, *"Your card has been declined!"* We humbly reply, "Can you try it again?" *"I've tried it three times!"* Baffled, we begin mumbling explanations about why or how this is happening.

Banks often put a hold on a card that has been used suspiciously. This action is made to stop further fraud on the account. When we try to use it, it may come back declined.

There's a thin line between needing grace and abusing it. If we abuse the account granted to us – the righteousness of Christ – it may not be in good standing. Reciting the *Sinner's Prayer* when we we're 12 doesn't give us a license to be reckless with our identity in Him.

APPRAISE REPORT

I've always found the notion that one could 'sell his soul' or 'gain the world but lose his soul' as ridiculously peculiar. The concept implies that a person is bribed with material excess. But the truth is, we often sell our souls for much less.

There's no need for the devil to overpay or even pay at all. The truth is, most of us don't need to gain the world to compromise our integrity, *we compromise it everyday.* Theoretically, the devil would only need to propose granting *everything* for one's soul if he didn't already have it. And he already does if we don't understand the value Christ puts on it.

THE UNGRATEFUL DEAD

We often fail to express gratitude when we have the opportunity to do so. Whether it be a job, a relationship, or the life of a loved one, we often realize how much we value something when we lose it. And what's the point of being grateful when it's too late?

When a man dies, it doesn't matter if he was good or bad; we speak well of him nonetheless. Even if he was a hitman mobster, on the day of his absence from this earth, the eulogist will say that he was a loving father. He was a man willing do anything for his family, including destroy other families. But if the deceased were an exceptionally good person, then people may dedicate a memorial to commemorate his life. *Too bad he isn't there to see it.* After all, what value does gratitude have to the dead?

"So I say to you: Ask and it will be given to you; seek and you will find; knock and the door will be opened to you." Luke 11:9

No matter how distant we may think we are from God, as long as we have the capacity to seek Him, He can be reached. But every day that we don't, our hearts harden. Once we have departed from this physical body, God will be completely absent. There will be no point of being grateful of His sacrifice then. After all, what value does the cross have to someone in hell?

Hell? *Ha!* It's seen as a religious fear tactic used to scare people into faith. A make-believe place where we're punished for the moral discrepancies of a past life. We think of a little red devil, two horns, and a pointed tail – *perhaps prodding us for eternity.*

If we think of hell as a fiery pit, we've completely missed the point. Hell is the absence of God, and the absence of anything *of* God. This includes, but is not limited to, the common grace that makes us relatively kind, loving, and peaceful to one another. Even on Earth, any good nature towards fellow man, is a reflection of God's nature.

SEPARATION ANXIETY

God created Adam in His own image. He created us to fellowship with Him, but we're separated by sin. As long as we're living, we have an opportunity to restore this fellowship; despite how far away we feel we are.

"About three in the afternoon Jesus cried out in a loud voice, 'Eli, Eli, lema sabachthani?' (which means 'My God, my God, why have you forsaken me?')." Matthew 27:46

When Christ died on the cross, He cried out in anguish. Not just because of the physical pain of being flogged, crowned with thorns, and crucified. The real anguish was the sin of the world He took upon Himself. He who knew no sin was completely separated from God on our behalf; *He was in hell.*

IS IGNORANCE BLISS OR MISS?

Imagine being relocated to a developing country, torn away from the luxuries that we consider to be basic to our existence – air-conditioning, hot showers, and the Internet. We may cry out in anguish and frustration. *"This is hell!"*

But as we look around, we realize no one else is concerned. Are the neighbors devastated about not having a dishwasher? *What is a dish?* Why aren't the village kids moping about their lack of video games, iPads, or cartoons? They may be suffering from other things, but not over the loss of something they're blissfully ignorant of.

Since we're born into a sinful nature, we've never experienced true fellowship with God. Only three people, Adam, Eve, and Jesus, have ever had an understanding of this connection, and then lost it. Jesus cried out when He was separated from God. As they mocked Him on the cross, His heart broke for them, "Forgive them Father, they know not what they do" (Luke 23:34).

We would cry out too, but we haven't lost anything that we know of. We aren't devastated about not having fellowship with God because we don't know what that really is. Is our ignorance bliss or miss?

SHAME ON ME

"For I am not ashamed of the gospel, because it is the power of God that brings salvation to everyone who believes: first to the Jew, then to the Gentile." Romans 1:16

The context of this verse was to encourage Christians who were living in a world that had never heard about Jesus. Christianity was seen as a cult, and it was tearing families apart. Parents often condemned new converts. Some were even being executed for their faith. Paul was telling them to be strong, to be unashamed.

Are we ashamed of the gospel? *We don't have to be!* We live in a country founded on Christian beliefs, as skewed as they may be. We don't have to fear that our family will reject us, or that our community will persecute us – unless of course, we consider our peers poking fun as persecution.

But here's the thing. It's not that I'm ashamed of the gospel of Christ, but of myself. I am ashamed of what we have done despite knowing the gospel. The early Christians died for Christ, while most of us are having trouble living for Him. By identifying ourselves as a Christians, we often bring shame to Jesus.

Peter was scared when he denied knowing Jesus three times. He loved Jesus, but he wasn't strong enough to identify himself with Him. He was afraid of losing his life. Peter lied out of fear; we lie out of ignorance. But our lie isn't that we, don't know Jesus. *It's that we do.* We think we do, but the truth is not in us.

I NEVER KNEW YOU

"Whoever says, 'I know Him,' but does not do what He commands is a liar, and the truth is not in that person." 1 John 2:4

If someone asks us if we're Christian, we usually say yes. After all, there's no real threat. In the West, our lives are not on the line, our churches are not being bombed, and our families are not being targeted. A person's true character is exhibited when the stakes are high; *fair-weather* makes it hard to distinguish. Some Christians are literally dying for something real, while we comfortably live for something fake.

As Comfortable Christians, we expect to inherit the kingdom of God even though our deeds are of the flesh. We are warned in Galatians 5:19 that these things will hinder us. We may not purposely ignore these verses, but the moral decay of our society eases our alarm to sin.

"Not everyone who says to me, 'Lord, Lord,' will enter the kingdom of heaven, but only the one who does the will of my Father who is in heaven." Matthew 7:21

"Depart from me; I never knew you," are the coldest words we could ever hear. Would we plead for mercy or try to jog God's memory of the times we went to church? Will He pull a lever that opens up the trap floor we're standing on? *Theoretically,* we should be relieved because we didn't really want God in life; *why would we want him in death?* Perhaps the eternal separation is mutual.

Tip

Prepare yourselves for the possibility of Jesus denying you with a rehearsed rebuttal. First, act very surprised. "What??!" Then, engage Him in some joking and pleasantries to lighten the mood – perhaps regarding His omnipresent, omnipotent, and omniscient status. There's no way He doesn't know us. And finally, if you have any religious tattoos, clothing, or accessories, *that would be the time* to reveal them. There's *no way* you will be sent to hell with Jesus tats!

Just because we know *of* Jesus, doesn't mean we *know* Jesus. Let's say we went to the White House expecting to have dinner with the President. If he says, "Depart from me; I never knew you," are we going to show him our 'Vote for President' T-shirts? Just because we know *of* him, doesn't mean we *know* him.

Will we be mad at ourselves, at the world, or at God? We'll have all of eternity to figure it out. When we think of Jesus, we think of children, lambs, and miracles. We conveniently forget His warnings. And for those who are eternally lost despite believing in Him, *how tragic will it be?* Would we still be grateful for the cross if He didn't accept us into the kingdom, or will we eternally be the ungrateful dead?

PART 6:
COMING OF AGE

CHEERS! TO ALL OF THE PASTORS:
A satirical letter

At this time, I would like to propose a toast to those who make Comfortable Christianity possible. Cheers! To all of the pastors who don't mention sin, or even better, downplay sin. After all, why dodge it when we can dismiss it — it's all covered in our comprehensive grace policy!

Thanks for teaching us how to be better people — in terms of purpose, passion, and prosperity — as opposed to being better disciples of Christ... unless of course, that discipleship somehow benefits us in terms of purpose, passion, and prosperity. After all, we delight in the Lord, so that He makes our lives delightful.

Whatever our ages, we have remained infants in Christ — sustained only by your regurgitation of the Word. Your charisma and charm is like a parent who makes airplane noises in an attempt to feed an unwilling baby. Thanks for accommodating to our pickiness with extra helpings of Jeremiah 29 and other 'plans and promises'.

With your help, we have cultivated an environment in which correcting our brothers and sisters is perceived of as being judgmental. *Off with the whistleblower's head!* We're so afraid of offending each other, that we offend God instead. Well played.

However, I do have a bone to pick with some of you. The one command given substantial importance is tithes and offerings. *This bites.* Especially when it seems that the only thing being "pressed down, shaken together and running over," are your pockets!

I would point out that Apostle Paul spread the gospel working as a layman so that he wouldn't financially burden those he ministered to, but ultimately, he burdened them with truth! *—that sly devil!*

Paul insisted that faith without works is dead. Like a bait and switch, he pulled us in with grace, and then stung us with a responsibility to become living sacrifices — crucified with Christ. Just referencing it gives me chills.

Jesus taught us that He was the tree, we are His branches. Our role is to abide in Him, and He will abide in us. But you, pastor, have become our tree. We abide in you; we are your branches. And with your aid, we've indefinitely postponed discipline.

I often wonder, have you comforted yourself with the same skewed faith that you have comforted us with, or are you a closet atheist making use your charisma? After all, being positive is good, but it's not the only thing.

Thank you, for making it the only thing.

When it's all said and done, I raise my glass to you. If it weren't for your misguidance, where would we be? After all, we probably wouldn't attend your service. Your pews would be empty, as would be your five-car garage! I guess we'd just have to find ourselves another to teach us "whatever our itching ears want to hear" (2 Timothy 4:3).

ELEMENTARY, MY DEAR

As a new father, I have been taking into account all of the behaviors and characteristics of my newborn son. He's completely helpless, and when he needs something, he depends on me to give it to him. For example, when he cries, I give him a pacifier. Eyes wide with excitement, he takes it and begins chomping away.

Chomp, chomp, chomp... *pluh!* He spits it out. And with a deafening cry, "Waaaaa!", he expresses his desire that I retrieve it. I oblige him, *over and over.*

I can't tell whether he sees me as a father or a pacifier retriever. But it's okay. One day he will have the neck control and coordination to get it himself, and ultimately, he'll grow out of it. Maybe he'll even become someone else's pacifier retriever. Until then, I'll fetch the pacifier – *renewing his joy and excitement.*

Chomp, chomp, chomp... *pluh!*

"Brothers and sisters, I could not address you as people who live by the Spirit but as people who are still worldly—mere infants in Christ." 1 Corinthians 3:1

No matter how many years we've been Christians, many of us are still infants in Christ. We cry for a good word! Then we rate the pastor on whether or not he gives us that punch. We're filled with joy and excitement. Chomp, chomp, chomp... and by Monday, *pluh!*

Waaaa! We have no spiritual neck control, no coordination, no ability to comfort ourselves with His word – let alone comfort someone else. Is God our father or pacifier retriever? One day we will mature, right?

JOKE OR LIE?

Like most people, I fancy my own sense of humor. What makes a joke funny is the same thing that makes a lie deceptive: truth. You begin with a bit of truth that all can relate to or agree with, and then deviate.

The one truth many Christians all agree on is that we would like to spiritually mature – especially after hearing an inspiring message. *But then we deviate.* Is our faith a joke, or a lie?

There's a certain excitement when the pastor is really feeding us, especially if we've been starving all week. We fail to realize that we're not followers of Jesus; we're followers of the pastor. And we rate him by his speaking performance, not his spiritual maturity.

We love great sermons. They make us feel like spiritually maturing. But do we seriously want to mature? Of course not.

When I examined my faith, I found that it wasn't genuine. Sure, I can't think of anyone better to resemble, to meditate on, and to persevere for, than Jesus Christ. That's the truth I keep deviating from. *Is my faith a joke or a lie?*

SUPERFICIAL MATURITY

I began writing this book when I realized that I *didn't really* want to spiritually mature. I was comfortable with the contradictions between my life and my faith – until I decided to stop deceiving to myself. That's when I began to examine hypocrisy through the eyes of a hypocrite.

Simultaneously, my church was asking me to speak and to lead Bible study – something I felt encouraged to do *because I was good at it.* One may refer to it as a gift. People began seeing my ability to consistently produce good messages as a sign that I was spiritually maturing. *They couldn't be further from the truth.*

Delivering a sermon is no more a sign of spiritual maturity that listening to it is.

When we serve the Lord in public, whether on the pulpit, the band, whatever – we get a 'good feeling.' People who see us serving may pat us on the back; they compliment and encourage us. *Then we deviate.* As we begin to associate the 'good feeling' with serving, if we're not careful, it begins to justify our sacrifice when we don't *feel* like serving. Likewise, for the listeners, the sacrifice was coming to church when they could be sleeping in, watching football, or going to brunch. If I do my job right, the listeners feel good – it begins to justify their attendance.

Would I serve if there were no good feelings justifying my effort? What if I felt unappreciated or unnoticed? You see, spiritual maturity doesn't rely on feelings.

I've found that it takes more spiritual maturity to clean up when no one is watching than to stand up on stage and deliver a fiery message. Perhaps that's why Jesus said that the first will be last, and the last will be first. Perhaps that's why spiritual leaders are warned that Jesus will tell them, "I never knew you."

Spiritual maturity doesn't materialize when someone makes use of the genetic predisposition, the talent, to speak well. (In my case, both of my parents are ministers.) It doesn't materialize when a worship leader makes use of the genetic predisposition to sing pitch perfect. Spiritual maturity is producing the fruit of the Spirit: love, joy, peace, patience, kindness, gentleness, and self-control (Galatians 5:22).

Spiritual maturity is how I treat my wife after the fiery sermon. Spiritual maturity is how we treat our co-workers, our neighbors, and our enemies. It's how we respond to negative situations. It's humility – sometimes the opposite of what we see in pastors, bishops, and prophets that profit. Spiritual maturity parallels our beliefs with our actions. It transforms us into the light of the world. *And there's nothing superficial about that.*

DEADBEAT LOSERS

"In fact, though by this time you ought to be teachers, you need some-one to teach you the elementary truths of God's word all over again."
Hebrews 5:12

We often reminisce about our childhood. Ahh, the good times when there were no real cares or responsibilities. Our parents clothed and fed us. We long to be kids again, to be free from the stress and responsibility of being an adult. We have no choice but to go to school, get a job, and sustain ourselves. Ideally, we'll get married and raise children — educating and nurturing them to maturity.

If you don't have a job, your daily routine may consist of pestering your parents for money, watching television, and complaining about the food selection in the fridge. *You blame everyone but yourself.* In addition, you don't attract anyone. Why would you? You're incapable of sustaining yourself, let alone providing for a future family.

Spiritual maturity is no different. Instead of being productive members and nurturing others, we get by as spiritual deadbeat losers. We live in our pastor's basement, complaining about the lack of breakthrough.

Spiritual deadbeats never attract anyone. After all, why would the world be attracted to our faith if it doesn't sustain us? The only people we attract are other deadbeats, other Comfortable Christians.

STAKEHOLDERS

"Jesus said, 'I am the true vine, and my Father is the gardener. He cuts off every branch in me that bears no fruit.'" John 15:1

This is a troubling verse about being an unproductive member of the kingdom. Jesus goes on to say that these branches wither away and are thrown into a fire. But note this, the word fire, as used in the original Hebrew text, translates as ... fire. *Yikes.* God wants us to bear fruit, to be productive, to advance the kingdom, or we will be cast away from Him! So what is a Comfortable Christian to do? *The bare minimum.*

Companies today are always trying to be efficient and boost their productivity. However, some employees may not be vested in a company's success. This is especially true in dead end jobs where upward mobility is limited or scarce. These employees spend their work hours complaining and wasting resources. Day in and day out, they do the bare minimum – just enough to not get fired.

But what about the company's department heads, managers, and co-owners? They have a vested stake in the success of the company and are constantly seeking growth and productivity. They often buy stock in the company. When it succeeds, they succeed. When the company loses, they lose. They're vested branches within the company.

"Now if we are children, then we are heirs of God and co-heirs with Christ, if indeed we share in his sufferings in order that we may also share in his glory." Romans 8:17

The kingdom is the same, in this respect. Some of us are non-invested servants who complain and waste the kingdom's resources. We are constantly being poured into, but there is no return on investment. *We're doing the bare minimum.* We have no stock in the God's kingdom. In fact, we may even have stock elsewhere. But we're all called to be leaders, to be stakeholders.

KNOW YO' ROLE

"The eye cannot say to the hand, 'I don't need you!' And the head cannot say to the feet, 'I don't need you!' On the contrary, those parts of the body that seem to be weaker are indispensable." 1 Corinthians 12:21-22

We all have different roles and abilities. Although some parts seem more important than others, we need the cooperation of all to function. No one is called to do nothing; no one's role is more important than another's. God does not esteem a pastor higher than an usher – even though we do. God has given us all gifts to be teachers, intercessors, healers, encouragers, and more.

We often overlook the powerful role of an encourager. Encouragement isn't Bible verse text spamming; it's a personal ministry. But if we're not spiritually maturing ourselves, then we don't even feel like encouraging others.

For example, a street bum isn't going to wake up bright and early on Monday morning to pat the backs of workers. He needs someone to pat his back. Likewise, we often come to church looking for a word of encouragement, *instead of being equipped to give one.* Those who are spiritually maturing are passionate about edifying others, not just themselves.

BUILDING BLOCK-ADES

Spiritual maturity is about serving, just as Christ came to serve. Now, one may ask himself, "I'm not a pastor, worship leader, or an usher – how can I serve?" I can think of some theoretical crap: feeding the homeless, mentoring fatherless children, or street ministry. They all sound commendable! But a better, reflective question is, "In what ways do I *avoid* or *overlook* serving?"

Home. The most basic, foundational level of serving begins here. How can I serve the world if I can't serve my family or my roommates? If the fruits of the Spirit aren't evident to the ones I'm nearest, how can they be to others? Unless, of course, I'm putting on a facade.

The problem with serving at home is we often feel unappreciated or unnoticed there. For example, if I washed the dishes and swept the floor, I'd want my wife to realize that *I washed the dishes and swept the floor!* If she didn't notice, *I'd be upset.* My service relies somewhat on a reward – being appreciated. We want to be seen when we're serving, even on the most basic level.

Is being appreciated too much to ask? Of course not. But since we associate serving with appreciation, we often look for a reward from man instead of God. We're conditioned since childhood to expect positive reinforcement. For example, we often received stickers, toys, and allowances for good behavior and good grades. In the workforce, employers reward us with merit badges, employee-of-the-month plaques, and raises.

But when we serve God, we may not get a physical reward. The blessings He gives us may not be material. A homeless man once told me he was "blessed and highly favored." You see, he understood that God's love for him has *nothing to do* with material wealth! *Or he was on drugs.*

On second thought, *he was definitely on drugs.*

Walking in the spirit is a lot like being on drugs. They're both an altered state of mind. Consider this, nothing can faze a crackhead. No home? *No problem!* Sounds like 'peace that surpasses understanding'! The question is, are we going to allow God to alter our state of mind?

Jesus once sat near the temple treasury and watched people put in offerings. Rich men dumped in large amounts and were publicly appreciated. However, Jesus cared more about a poor widow's offering. She tossed in two measly, worthless cents. No priest ran to her and said, "Thank you for your contribution." Her offering was seemingly unnoticed. *But Jesus noticed her.* In fact, he said, "This poor widow has put more into the treasury than all the others" (Mark 12:43). Serving God isn't about getting rewarded, acknowledged, or blessed. It takes an altered state of mind – one that doesn't rely on human reinforcement.

"Serve wholeheartedly, as if you were serving the Lord, not people, because you know that the Lord will reward each one for whatever good they do." Ephesians 6:7-8

In theory, serving should receive appreciation; but it must not be dependent on it. This is a point where Christians should differ from unbelievers. Everyone loves people who love them back – who appreciate them. But Christ called us to love and serve those who don't love and appreciate us. I'm not sure if I want that. *Do you?*

Jesus prayed for the forgiveness of those who crucified Him. I would've prayed, "Father, strike them!" Before we can serve others, we must be able to serve on the elementary level – *the home.*

BE CONSUMED

How can I pray, "God, guide my life," if I don't let Him guide my day? And how can I pray, "God, guide my day," if I don't let him guide my hour? Coming of age in Christ begins with the basic understanding that He must consume all of me.

To fulfill our potential in Christ, to reach spiritual maturity, we must prepare ourselves to be consumed. We must first ripen – *just like a fruit.* When selecting fruit in a grocery store, we pick carefully, noting its ripeness. If it's not ready yet, we expect it to be soon.

Then we wait.

But what if the fruit never ripens? Imagine a bundle of bananas in the kitchen that remained green, week after week. We may want to eat them, but they're not ready. Likewise, God can only consume us if we're willing to mature. He'll never force us to ripen.

THE BREAKDOWN

When we consume food, there is a three-step process. First, the food is chewed, broken down, and swallowed. Second, our bodies extract vitamins, minerals, and proteins that help to sustain us. Lastly, whatever is not useful is excreted.

When God consumes us, we're first broken down and humbled. We understand that everything we do is for Him and through Him. He extracts our qualities, gifts, and talents for His purposes (Romans 12:6). This sustains the body of Christ, producing growth and strength. Finally, whatever is bad for the body is excreted.

We often try to excrete things from ourselves before coming to Jesus and being broken down. *That's His job, not ours.* It would be like trying to discard the food material that becomes poop *before we eat it.* All God requires of us is to be humble and willing.

PREY OR PREDATOR?

"Therefore let us move beyond the elementary teachings about Christ and be taken forward to maturity, not laying again the foundation of repentance from acts that lead to death, and of faith in God." Hebrews 6:1

Whether prey or predator, a newborn infant of any species is extremely vulnerable. Even the most fearsome animals – alligators, lions, or snakes – are susceptible to being easily snuffed out. For this reason, there's a sense of urgency to develop quickly.

On the other hand, we humans lack the urgency. In fact, the more civilized we become, the less urgency we have. For example, in war-torn or disease-plagued regions, a 10-year-old may have to take care of his siblings. Meanwhile, in America, we expect our parents to buy us a car, pay our college tuition, and even let us move back in if we don't find a job. We mature slower because there's no physical threat, no sense of urgency.

Likewise, our spiritual maturity is slow because we don't see a spiritual threat. For many of us, there's virtually no sense of urgency. We're blind to the demonic influences behind secular music, environments, and relationships. We're mere infants in Christ – susceptible to being easily snuffed out.

When we become spiritually mature, not only do we become a difficult target for the enemy; *we begin to target the enemy*. It's elementary, my dear. Instead of becoming ensnared in sin, we help others overcome it. But the devil does not intend to let us reach this age. Like a cat that toys with its prey, he toys with us as we revert to relearning the foundation of repentance – *the struggle of a guilty conscience.*

GUILTY CONSCIENCE

"It needs a good man to repent. And here comes the catch. Only a bad person needs to repent: only a good person can repent perfectly. The worse you are the more you need it and the less you can do it. The only person who could do it perfectly would be a perfect person – and he would not need it." -C.S. Lewis

A guilty conscience can makes us feel distant from God. It points out our faults, not to rectify them, but rather to create separation. It makes us feel unworthy of God's presence, grace, and love – *things we were never worthy of in the first place.* In fact, the Word says that our righteousness is as filthy rags.

There are two types of guilt:
1) Godly sorrow, which leads to repentance.
2) Condemnation, which leads away from it.

Let's begin with the latter.

CONDEMNATION NATION

"Therefore, there is now no condemnation for those who are in Christ Jesus." Romans 8:1

God is faithful and just to forgive us, but we often over-rule Him and condemn ourselves. It's not as blatant as appealing an acquittal: "No, your Honor! I swear I'm guilty!" But because we feel sinful, we separate ourselves from prayer, worship, and fellowship. We cut ourselves away from the very things that edify us.

A sense of condemnation may build up within us, only to fizzle out into spiritual numbness. We realize how far we've strayed ... and then we accept it. We no longer feel the guilt be-cause we've become spiritually insensitive. In this manner, con-demnation makes us drift further and further away from God.

Judas Iscariot experienced the anguish of condemnation when he betrayed Jesus. He was disgusted, ashamed, and convicted. And his guilty conscience led him to suicide.

Some say Jesus would have forgiven him, but Judas may have not been able forgive himself. After all, condemnation tries to overrule our sanctification through the cross. It rewrites our favorite hymns, saying, "What can wash away our sins? *Nothing,* not even the blood of Jesus."

In contrast, the Apostle Peter experienced godly sorrow. After swearing to protect Jesus, he denied him three times. But his conviction didn't lead him to condemnation.

Just by staying alive, he allowed himself to accept Christ's forgiveness. We can either let the knowledge of our sin kill our spiritual lives, or strive towards restoration. Godly sorrow says, "Go and sin no more," while condemnation says, "You're screwed up. You might as well keep on sinning."

CLEARING OUR CONSCIENCE

"How much more, then, will the blood of Christ, who through the eternal Spirit offered himself unblemished to God, cleanse our conscience from acts that lead to death, so that we may serve the living God?" Hebrews 9:14

God not only wants to forgive us, but to also clear our consciences. Otherwise, we would be unable to serve Him. We're called *the righteousness of Christ,* and seeing ourselves as *anything less* is undermining His sacrifice. Yet somehow, we find it easier to die spiritually than to move forward.

Have you ever been forgiven of betraying a friend, but *you* couldn't let it go? If you keep beating yourself up, the relationship can never be the same. Instead of working to restore what was lost, you avoid the person. Likewise, condemning ourselves of sin makes us avoid a relationship with God. We never get as close as we once were.

FEAR OF HYPOCRISY

When people are asked why they don't attend church, many times they say there are too many hypocrites. *We all hate hypocrites.* Even Jesus didn't like them! (Although He loved them by default). He called the religious leaders 'white washed tombs,' beautiful on the outside, but dead and unclean on the inside.

We dislike hypocrites so much, we're afraid of being them. And nothing is more hypocritical than coming to church on Sunday, *hours after a sinful Saturday.* Our logical response is to not come, especially if alcohol is still oozing out of our pores. We avoid hypocrisy at all costs, *even salvation.*

Granted, going to church doesn't equate to attaining salvation any more than training for a marathon will mean we'll complete it. However, it's highly unlikely that we'll finish the race if we don't train. So what can we do about this hypocritical situation? We can either: a) continue going to church and repent, b) continue going to church without repenting, or c) stop going to church.

In fear of being hypocrites, we often avoid God completely. We feel Him tugging on our hearts, but we suppress Him; eventually He'll stop. Our hearts harden as we convince ourselves that we'll find our way... *after* we clean up our lives.

SAVE YOUR APOLOGIES

There are three types of apologies: 1) sorry I got caught, 2) sorry I offended you, and 3) sorry for my action. We may not truthfully regret our actions, but we must appear to – *to smooth things over.* No one will be able to tell, unless of course, we keep repeating the offense.

Sometimes we ask God to forgive us *just* to clear our mind, to smooth things over with Him. After all, we're going to need to apologize before we ask for blessings, *duhhh!* But if we keep seeking forgiveness for the same things, are we really sorry?

Picture yourself apologizing for cheating on your significant other. If you're not being genuine, all you're really saying is: "Honey, I'm so sorry you caught me cheating. I should have been sneakier," or, "Honey, I'm so sorry that my cheating offended you."

The key in an effective apology is not just to sound genuine, but to be genuine! *Surprise!* You may manage to smooth things over the first time, but if you repeat the transgression, it will be clear that your previous apology was insincere. And fake apologies hurt more than they help.

When we find ourselves apologizing to God for the same thing over and over, are we being genuine? We may soon realize that we don't hate sin, but rather, *apologizing for sin.* Who, but perhaps ourselves, are we fooling? Let's save our fake apologies. After all, what we're really saying is: "God, I'm so sorry You're omniscient. If only there was some way I could hide this from You," or, "God, I'm sorry my sin offends You."

KEEP PUMPING

We all have guilt. Like cholesterol, guilt can be good or bad. For example, HDL cholesterol clears our arteries and helps to fight against heart disease. On the other hand, LDL cholesterol builds plaque in our arteries. Many people don't realize their (bad) cholesterol is high until they've suffered a stroke – *blood has been blocked.*

Godly sorrow keeps us pumping, clearing the flow of His communion, which is our salvation. On the other hand, condemnation slowly builds up until His blood has been completely blocked. We don't even realize that inner guilt is killing us. We think we're fine.

Since bad cholesterol is linked to diet, it often correlates with obesity. It's apparent that overweight individuals are at a high risk for a heart attack, but slim people can be too. In fact, it's much more deceptive. Likewise, it's obvious that a Christian who is visibly faltering may be feeling condemned, but this can also be the case for someone who is in regular church attendance. Ultimately, the acknowledgement of our sin will either draw us closer to Him, or push us further away.

ACCEPTING ADDICTION

Everyone has fought addiction. We like to point out the common ones like alcohol, drugs, or porn. But the truth is, addiction can be gossip, greed, work, gluttony, sex, television, social media, social media, or even social media.

We love our addictions, and being free of them isn't what we really want. But sometimes our addictions become so powerful that we have no choice but to recognize them. It's clear to us, and possibly others, that it's preventing our growth.

This concession, however, is not the end. And the path to deliverance may seem like a futile effort.

 The easiest way to end your struggle with addiction is to deny it exists. If you feel that addressing addiction doesn't really apply to you, then you are on the right track! There's nothing that *consistently* comes between you and God! *Ok, maybe something.* But it's not that serious, right? It's not an *'addiction'*; it's just something you aren't ready to give up right now. Denial is the first step in maintaining addiction. *What addiction?* Perfect!

ENVIRONMENTAL HAZARDS

It amazes us when we hear of someone quitting an addiction cold turkey. We'd prefer to wean ourselves off, progressing at our own *dismal* pace. Let's say we're trying to quit smoking. After a week of abstinence, we *deserve* a cigarette! Let's say our struggle is with gluttony. After a rigorous sit-up, we *deserve* a cheeseburger! Likewise, we often celebrate victory with a defeat.

Going cold turkey requires complete avoidance of situations that may be tempting. It stipulates a change of environment, to avoid potential hazards. For example, if our struggle were alcoholism, then we would have to avoid bars and even social gatherings where alcohol is present. Even sparkling apple cider can prove to be a death knell! But c'mon, we don't want to be that guy who won't drink *just one* because we can't handle it. Geez, show some willpower.

DO IT YOURSELF

We often try to break addiction with willpower. It's fairly ineffectual, enabling us to continue enjoying it. Honestly, it's what we *really* wanted anyway. No matter how hard we try, we're almost *guaranteed* to fail. The spirit is willing, but the flesh is weak. In fact, we may fail so much that we stop trying! *Acceptance.*

Attempting to break an addiction alone only serves to silence our spirit. We tell ourselves it's a work in progress, as if to quiet the inquiry of when the progress will actually materialize.

FREEDOM FACADE

The *Emancipation Proclamation* freed all the slaves after the Civil War. Let's imagine that we have been slaves since birth. But one day, the Union troops march into the plantation and tell us that we're free! The enemy has been defeated! We're free!

We're celebrating, singing hallelujah! We begin to pack our bags ... oh, we don't have bags. We grab our money ... oh, we don't have money. *Whatever!* We're free to go!

But where to?

Imagine the joy, the excitement, and the sense of liberation ... only to be curbed with the realization that we have nowhere to go. *Slavery is all we know.* As a result, sharecropping or tenant farming – which is supposedly 'free market' labor – becomes widespread.

With open arms, our former slave masters graciously accept our plea for reinstatement. The only thing that changed for us was our title, *freedmen*. Heh, yeah, right.

"But now that you know God – or rather are known by God – how is it that you are returning back to those weak and miserable forces? Do you wish to be enslaved by them all over again?" Galatians 4:9

All mankind is born into slavery to sin. But Jesus defeated the enemy; He was tortured and crucified so that we may be emancipated! *Hallelujah!* We're free from the bondage of sin and dea ... *uhhh, wait,* why are we still sinning?

We're freedmen, yet still oppressed by the same masters, the same addictions. The only thing that has changed for many of us is our title, *Christians*. Heh, yea, right.

Being set free doesn't mean we'll stay free. An impure spirit can't possess a Christian, but it can oppress one. Even after the bondage is broken, the spirit will try to return. If it finds one is unoccupied, it becomes an easy target for recapture (Matthew 12:44).

To stay free, we must be occupied by the Holy Spirit and the word of God. It's the only strength to overcome sin. When Jesus was being tempted in the wilderness, He responded each time with 'it is written.'

ACCOUNTABILITY COUNTS

"No temptation has overtaken you except what is common to man." 1 Corinthians 10:13

Although we struggle with different things, no addiction is a different or special case. Someone has overcome the same thing we're wrestling with. The Word encourages us to tell a brother or sister in Christ about our struggles; we're not alone in this battle (James 5:16). Sin can only thrive in darkness. By sharing our weaknesses, we expose them to the light. This liberates us. Intercession and accountability are key.

There are three major fears when it comes to opening up about an addiction:

1) **The fear of gossip.** The last thing we want is for our struggle to be the trending topic of the congregation. For example, "Did you hear that Brother Jermaine is struggling with crack-cocaine addiction? Pray for him."

2) **The fear of being identified by the addiction.** We assume every time people think of us, they think of us *addicted*. For example, "Hello Brother Jermaine. How's your crack-cocaine addiction?"

3) **The greatest fear, however, is actually being free.**

Imagine how hard it would be to enjoy an addiction *under the threat* of being held accountable. But we can't win all the battles in our lives alone. We need the love and support of each other.

When Joshua was fighting the Amalekites, God commanded Moses to keep his staff up. When he lowered his arms out of fatigue, Israel began to lose. He couldn't keep his arms raised with his own strength, so Aaron and Hur held him steady until sunset. Who is holding you steady, and who are you holding steady?

INTIMACY ISSUES

Nowadays, people often worry about being cheated on. Is she talking to an ex? Is he really working late? But before stressing ourselves out, monitoring texts the *suspect* has with others, monitor the communication he/she has with you. There's usually a decline in communication.

Also, it's very difficult for a cheater to keep the level of intimacy consistent. Rarely does a man have the same enthusiasm to make love to his wife after a long day of making love to his secretary. Even if he fulfills his spousal duties, it may not be with the same... *fervor.* The lack of communication and intimacy are red flags.

"Come near to God and he will come near to you." James 4:8

It's often said, "Christianity is not a religion; it's a relationship." Have you ever taken into consideration what kind of jacked up relationship we're in? We're not on the 'Rock'; *we're on the rocks!* There's little communication and little intimacy.

If we're not drawing near to God, then we're pulling away – we're more likely to be in communion with the flesh. Sure, we may fulfill our Christian duties – go to church, even read the Word – but not with the same enthusiasm in which we'd hang out with friends, go to the movies, or gossip about people who hang out with friends and go to movies.

Intimacy is a major player in the success of any relationship. When married couples are being counseled, they're often asked how frequently they're intimate. Some say it has been days, weeks, or months. Others are convinced that they're practicing celibacy.

It's one thing to be with a person, and it's another thing to be *one with a person.* If a couple shares the same desires, interests, and goals, they will continue to grow together. Their intimacy may become so high that it becomes difficult, or rather, *undesirable* to cheat.

"Submit yourselves to God, resist the devil, and he will flee from you." James 4:7

We're familiar with the second half of this verse, but often fail to see the importance of submittal. If we're not intimate with God, we can't resist the devil. In fact, we don't want to. The closer we are to Him, the more difficult, or rather, undesirable it becomes to sin.

Imagine how impossible it would become to enjoy our addictions if we were drawing near to God. Could we tolerate lust, drunkenness, lying, cheating, and gossiping as we worship? We'd probably need some space from Him.

The line, "I need some space," prefixes a breakup. It's not a flat out rejection, but rather, a step back. It's either a time of reassessment, or a time to *wild out!* You can do whatever you want; *you submit to no one.*

Going to Las Vegas this weekend? Don't forget to tell Jesus, "I need some space." Don't worry Lord, it's not a breakup, just a step back.

In marriage, there's little space. Couples are constantly held accountable by their spouses. Many people try to 'get their demons out' while they're young, and then settle down. But there's one last act of unaccountability prior to marriage: the bachelor/bachelorette party. A 'don't ask, don't tell' policy is in full effect! We'll never have this much space again – unless we divorce. But we don't want to *divorce* Jesus. We just want an 'open relationship.'

If we're constantly in prayer – worshipping and seeking God – there's no room for sin. God is referred to as a consuming fire. The closer we get to Him, the more He will refine us, burning away our impurities. But we must desire Him from the heart.

THE HEART OF THE ISSUE

"You have heard that it was said, 'You shall not commit adultery.' But I tell you that anyone who looks at a woman lustfully has already committed adultery with her in his heart." Matthew 5:27-28

Much of the conversation guys have from the moment they hit puberty until they croak in a nursing home is in regards to, *what they would do to that girl walking by*, given, her improbable consent. The next conversation is usually in regards to what they would do to the *next* girl walking by. As Christian guys, we either partake in this imaginary conquest, or just stay oddly quiet as the conversation moves on to another topic, the *next next* girl.

Jesus dropped a bomb on these guys by telling them looking at a woman with lust counts the same as committing adultery, bringing new meaning to the term, 'one minute man.' Until then, they thought as long as they didn't act on their lust, they didn't commit a sin.

Imagine if criminals were caught before they committed a crime, because they had done it in their hearts. What if the film, *Ocean's 11* ended in fifteen minutes, the police arresting the heist conspirators as they drew up a plan. No longer needing 'means, motive, and opportunity' to prove guilt, the judge has a heart detector test. And unlike a lie detector test, trying to cheat it only *alerts it even more!* We would completely be free of crime, and completely free of people to commit them.

The heart of the issue is not our actions; it's our desires.

This whole *heart adultery* thing is a true bummer because it takes away the issue of technicalities. *Technically*, we don't steal everything we envy. *Technically*, we don't bow down to our shoe collections. *Technically*, we're not sleeping with Playboy bunnies or Christian Grey.

THE CHOPPING BLOCK

"And if your right eye causes you to stumble, gouge it out and throw it away ... And if your right hand causes you to stumble, cut it off and throw it away. It is better for you to lose one part of your body than for your whole body to be thrown into hell." Matthew 5:29-30

Picture yourself pick-pocketing in a third world country where the punishment for theft is the chopping off of hands. It's the ultimate, 'go and sin no more!' Be grateful: you've been saved from hellfire! You'll enter the kingdom of heaven like, "Look Pa, no hands!"

You can never steal again because you've lost your eye-hand coordination. But that doesn't mean you won't *desire* to steal again.

Eye-hand coordination refers to the coordinated control of eye and hand movement. Without it, it would be impossible to do simple tasks like picking up a book, dialing a phone number, or hacking into the CIA. God's issue with us isn't our actions, but how our heart controls our actions. We can refer to it as *heart-hand* coordination. Our hands only reach out for what our hearts have desired.

Aha! So the part we should be cutting out is our heart! *Scalpel*, please.

Jesus wasn't promoting the idea of self-mutilation – much to the dismay to those prepared to fulfill the literal suggestion. Rather, He was expressing how serious sin that goes unchecked could be. It would be better to lose parts of our physical body, than to lose our spiritual self.

But Comfortable Christianity doesn't address addiction; *it accepts it.* It may take a couple steps forward, but it ultimately falls short of freedom. It limits itself. Freedom was never the heart's true desire. What we truly love is whatever we're addicted to.

I AM THE LIMIT

When something comes along that can revolutionize the way we do things, we say, *"the sky is the limit"*. It means that the possibilities are endless; the impact is immeasurable. For example, the introduction of the Internet has made gaining information limitless. We're no longer restricted to our education, our libraries, and our news outlets – *all of which are controlled by the government.* Because of this, some countries recognize the Internet as a threat. Their citizens may be able to access Google, but their searches render limited results.

The Old Covenant, which was simply rules and sacrifices, only brought death. It couldn't save us; it only condemned our actions. In addition, it required an animal sacrifice to atone for sin. Jesus revolutionized the covenant by becoming the sacrifice: He bridged the connection between God and man. His will is to empower us with the Spirit: *to make the sky the limit.*

Our flesh recognizes this New Covenant as a threat to its control. *Oh,* it's fine with us going to church, reading the Word, and even praying regularly. Its main concern is *repressing our transformation.* The flesh prefers that we operate the old way, in order to limit our fellowship with God – so it's no longer the sky, but rather, I am the limit.

THE COMFORTABLE CHRISTIAN MANIFESTO

"Therefore do not let sin reign in your mortal body so that you obey its evil desires." Romans 6:12

When a dictator or a political party reigns over a country, they take certain measures to ensure the longevity of their rule. There's a no tolerance policy for any opposition. There's no 'freedom of the press' – and critical journalists *magically disap-*

pear. No citizen can vote, petition, or protest a reigning authority without the fear of imprisonment or death.

Likewise, when we allow the flesh to reign within us, any protest by the spirit man is quickly suppressed. And although we may not allow the flesh reign, we don't allow the spirit to rule either. As Comfortable Christians, we try to cater to both parties.

Comfortable Christianity is a bipartisan approach. And for years, even decades, we're stuck in deadlocked congress. Nothing gets done; there's no spiritual maturity. And that right there – the stalling of progress – is good enough for the flesh. Its campaign goals can be summed up in a manifesto:

Worship God, *on Sundays.* Have the Passion of Christ, *on DVD.* Encounter Jesus at a retreat, *but don't surrender.* God is love, *all we need is love.* You're not going to be perfect, *so don't strive to be.* Christianity is a relationship; *relationships need compromise.* Seek God's heart, *so His hands will follow.* Seek God's kingdom, *after you've established yours.* Delight in the Lord, *if He gives you the desires of your heart.* And remember, faith without works *is still faith.*

MISSION UNACCOMPLISHED

Becoming victorious is rarely a single event. A country doesn't win a war with a single air-strike, a boxer rarely wins a fight with the first blow, and a sprinter never wins a race with the first hurdle. Victory is about consistently winning the little battles, moment by moment, until the engaged party has come under submission.

It's also important to know who the enemy is. For example, when New York was attacked on 9/11, the good ol' U.S. of A. was ready to strike back – *but strike whom?* Well, we unleashed our wrath on Iraq. And after the initial attack, our military raised a banner that boasted, "Mission Accomplished." *Victory!* But they had no weapons of mass destruction.

I once saw a viral video of a student flicking his sleeping classmate's ear from behind. The victim vengefully rose up and ripped off his shirt. His bodily language vividly expressed, *"I declare war!"* Then he sucker punched an innocent bystander – or subsequently, a by-sleeper. *Victory!* The actual culprit was unscathed, free to flick another day.

When we fail to realize who the enemy is, our efforts are futile. Oftentimes, the last person we hold accountable is ourselves. For example, there was a time when I was over 30 percent body fat. I pondered how I became so overweight. I blamed the fast-food chains and my busy schedule. I tried to lose weight, but I never won the victory until I realized that *I* was to blame.

Once I realized that I was my own worst enemy – that a part of me, the glutton, was hurting a more important part, my health – I declared war correctly. I won victory over myself by winning the little battles, moment by moment, meal by meal.

This *self-enemy* is what Christianity refers to as *the flesh*. It comes from within, and if we try to blame our spiritual failures on others – the media, our friends, or the devil (as in "the devil made me do it") – we have focused on the wrong enemy. We leave *the flesh* free to live another day.

The reason why Jesus told us to crucify the flesh daily is because the only way to walk in victory is to recognize it as our enemy. We often make enemies out of our neighbors, co-workers, or families, when the real source of our anger, lust, and pride is from within. We must all come to the realization that "I am the limit; I am hurting me." The true enemy of the Spirit is me – I must come under God's submission.

Our flesh does a great job convincing us that we're not that bad. For example, I could have rationalized my weight – as most Americans are overweight, too. We're convinced that we're generally good people (despite the fact that we are motivated by material lust, sexual lust, and pride). But if Jesus rebutted being called 'good teacher,' affirming that no one is good but God alone, on what foundation is it that we rationalize ourselves? (Mark 10:18). The Apostle Paul, who we hold in the highest esteem, said, "What a wretched man I am! Who will rescue me from this body that is subject to death?" (Romans 7:24)

RULES OF ENGAGEMENT

"If you then, though you are evil, know how to give good gifts to your children, how much more will your Father in heaven give the Holy Spirit to those who ask Him!" Luke 11:13

A parent is expected to satisfy a child's needs, but not necessarily their desires. This is especially true if the desire doesn't even originate from them. For example, if a 5-year-old girl requests a BB gun, we can assume that the desire originated from someone else. In the same way, when we engage God with our desires, we must examine whether they're of the spirit or the flesh.

It's through the spirit that we're sons and daughters of God; the flesh has no communion. When our prayers fail to be consistent with the spirit, it becomes obvious that the flesh is in control. It's not only dictating how we live, but how we pray and ultimately, our connection with the Holy Spirit.

In order for God to transform us, we must allow Him to transform why we communicate with Him. We often treat Him like a celestial sugar daddy! Whether we toss up erratic prayers or steadily stream a laundry list of naming-and-claiming, our relationship with Him often revolves around the fulfillment of our flesh.

AN 'F' FOR EFFORT

To some extent, we subdue the desires of our flesh, trading them in for their spiritual counterparts. Instead of indulging in pride, possessions, and lust, we try to fulfill ourselves with humility, selflessness, and love. *But who are we fooling?* We're only churning out as many fruits of the Spirit as our flesh allows.

Consider this: a lion can't quench the instinctual desire for flesh at a vegan restaurant. Even if he tried, perhaps going as far as ordering the 'safari salad,' he'd still fantasize about eating the waitress. And if he finally succumbs, he'll cry out to God. "Why can't I stop?"

"He must increase, but I must decrease." John 3:30

We must understand the difference between *not wanting to commit sin* and *not wanting sin itself*. Oftentimes, we don't want to sin *because* it has been labeled 'sin.' But we may desire it just as much as a non-believer.

Instead of trying to correct our desires, why not depend on God to transform them? It's a change that comes as result of His increase from within, *not of our own strength*. Anything short of this is compromise; it's an attempt to facilitate an environment where both God *and I* can increase.

We can't overthrow the flesh on our own. When we try to, it looks pathetic. All we can do is draw near to God, and He will draw near to us. It's as if He sees our willingness and increases our strength. The only thing limiting us is a half-baked attempt.

CLEARANCE THROUGH PERSEVERANCE

"We know that suffering produces perseverance; perseverance, character, and hope." Romans 5:3-4

We don't have to be perfect to glorify God. In fact, He's glorified more through our suffering. And there's no greater suffering than crucifying the flesh every day. Our constant wrestle with the flesh produces perseverance. The more we wrestle, the stronger we become – *even when we lose.*

A brother in Christ once shared a hilarious testimony. The Holy Spirit had convicted him because he lied to his boss about being on break. Instead of snuffing out his guilty conscience, he snitched on himself!

I chuckled. The Holy Spirit could never convict me of such a silly sin! Sure, his character amazed me. He was allowing God to purge him to the point where he couldn't get away with a *petty lie.* But that's not what I wanted.

It reminded me of something my mother once said, "Everyone [Christians] loves Jesus, but not everyone has character."

Consider the way we may tell a beggar that we don't have any cash, *even if we do.* It's technically a lie. Do you *really* want God to convict you of lying – to the point where you would go back and confess? "Forgive me beggar; *I lied.* I do have cash, but I'm still not going to give it to you." *You see,* there's gotta be a limit!

We often limit righteousness. We draw the line when it comes to how far we're going to allow God to purge us. We quell the Spirit when we ignore the conviction. Ultimately, our hope lies in God's willingness to not only make up for our inability, but also, *our lack of perseverance.*

THE FRESH ODOR

Few things can curb the satisfaction of stepping out of the shower. We feel so fresh, so clean. I was once indulging in the moment, in the fragrance of my own cleanliness, when it happened – *I farted.*

Is there anything worse than a post-shower fart? Just when we feel clean, nice and good about ourselves, *out slips a stench!* The subsequent mix of contrasting scents gives birth to an even more nauseating odor. The fart smells much worse than it would have if I had not showered at all.

Likewise, the moment we take pride in our submission to God, we're no longer submitting. Our perceived holiness becomes a filthy stench. There's always more work to be done in us. We will never be perfect. *But it's important that we strive for it.* An odd concept, yes. But it's what our faith calls for. Jesus told the Pharisees, if they could see, then their guilt would remain (John 9:41).

LONG LIVE THE KING

"The weapons we fight with are not the weapons of the world. On the contrary, they have divine power to demolish strongholds ... we take captive every thought to make it obedient to Christ." 2 Corinthians 10:4-5

When the flesh begins to lose control, we can smell its desperation. It goes into frenzy trying to commit sin – anything to let it live. But we've been given divine power to demolish strongholds and seize every thought, to bring ourselves into submission of the spirit's reign.

Our spirits may seem strong, empowered by a renewed desire, and finally a new ability. But we must close the deal and kill the flesh, *everyday.* Even if it seems too weak to do any harm.

In the *Lion King*, Scar pleads for mercy when Simba overthrows him. Even after knowing the truth – that Scar reigned as a result of killing his father – Simba lets him live. After all, Scar was now weak and harmless, right? Scar sprung back upon him, right after falsely conceding, "Long live the king!" He was never going to go in peace.

Let's not sit back and take satisfaction in the moment we feel victorious in Christ (Usually after a fiery sermon). Sure, the tables may have turned, but they can turn again. Jesus commanded us to kill the flesh everyday, because it will not go in peace. Anything short of this will allow its inevitable resurgence. Ultimately, it's up to us to be the flesh's limit.

UNDER THE INSPIRATION

Inspiration is the action or power of moving the intellect or emotions (Merriam-Webster). We love to be inspired by quotes, speakers, and stories. Even our fortune cookies have evolved into inspirational gurus. We 'think and grow rich' with every bite of orange chicken.

Many people even attribute their personal achievements to some sort of inspiration. We love to share what inspires us – posting uplifting sayings or retweeting things we think our friends will be inspired by.

Inspired to further research the definition of inspiration, I found that it's the act of influence. Influence is the source of inspiration. So instead of seeking a bit of divine inspiration, wouldn't it be better to seek divine influence? After all, inspiration only lasts so long. *But wait,* what exactly is influence?

Influence is the act or power of producing an effect without apparent exertion of force or direct exercise of command (Merriam-Webster). We may be aware of someone or something's influence, but what makes it so powerful is that we may not realize how strong it has become.

INSPIRATION VS. INFLUENCE

The term 'liquid courage' refers to the way alcohol has loosened our fears, producing a slightly skewed perception of potential consequence. Perhaps we'll approach a love interest who is clearly out of our league. Or maybe we'll tell our bosses how to do their jobs. We can refer to it as being 'under the inspiration' of alcohol.

We inspire each other with a shot of this or a toast of that. However, there are limits to the amount of 'inspiration' one can have before it becomes socially unacceptable. Too much inspiration can lead to being under the influence, which is discouraged... even by the likes of Captain Morgan (at least in his spiced rum commercials).

Being *under the influence* refers to a force stronger than our own taking over our ability to do things. Many times, it refers to the way alcohol inhibits our ability to drive, work, *or most importantly,* drink more! The more the *influence* has taken over, the less we are able to assess its grasp on us.

For example, a drunken man may claim to his friends that he's sober enough to drive home, downplaying the amount of influence he's under. A suspecting officer may pull him over and require him to do a sobriety test. "I've only had two beers," the driver claims while stumbling out of his seat. It becomes apparent that he's under the influence as he struggles to do simple tasks like walk a straight line, touch his nose, or reach for the officer's gun.

The same rule applies when we're under the influence of Christ. Everything we say and do will be affected by His influence. People will take note of the irregularities in our behavior.

Sure, everyone likes someone who is 'God inspired.' Our elected officials wouldn't stand a chance without claiming that they're Christian, attend church, and pray regularly. It's only when someone is 'God influenced' that they lose their appeal to society.

Likewise, our co-workers, neighbors, and friends love it when we're under the inspiration of God. There is no law against love, joy, peace, etc. (Galatians 5:23). But when we are under God's influence, immersed and intoxicated by Him, well, we've had *a little too much* Jesus.

MO' JESUS, MO' PROBLEMS

When we're intoxicated, we run into a myriad of problems. If we're drunk in public, we may get a ticket. If we go to work, we may get fired. If we drive, we may get arrested. There's no hiding that we reek of alcohol. We may not even care to try. Even after a shower, the stench may still ooze out of our pores.

Likewise, when we're intoxicated with Jesus, when we're under His influence, we run into issues as well. The world discourages this level of intoxication. To them, we reek of Christ. As His servants, they will hate us just like they hated Him.

"If the world hates you, keep in mind that it hated me first. If you belonged to the world, it would love you as its own ... A servant is not greater than his master. If they persecuted me, they will persecute you also." John 15:18-20

In our younger years the approval of our social circle is of great importance. Actually, *it's the only importance.* Christian values like abstinence are teased in middle and high school – especially if you're a guy. *"You're waiting for marriage?!?!* Ha-ha-ha! Hey everyone, look at this guy! *He's waiting for marriage!"* (A marriage that may ultimately end in divorce!). Blessing our food at lunch, praying at the flagpole, or joining a Bible club can make us look like... well, Jesus freaks.

Jesus warned that His followers would face persecution, and although the apostles are respected for experiencing the most brutal abuses, the *ruthless snickering* of our peers is nothing to scoff at!

Since we're social beings, we want to feel a sense of belonging. We like Christ, but we like *being liked* even more. We don't want to disrupt the social norms that would single us out. We don't want to be different; *we just want to be comfortable.*

UNDER OLD MANAGEMENT

As Comfortable Christians, we love to be *inspired* every Sunday morning. We sit in service anticipating a positive word. It gives us the strength we need to go on for hours! We toast each other with key points, briefly fellowshipping about how effective it would be if we applied it. A *Hallelujah Martini,* shaken not stirred. We love to be inspired by God, but not to be influenced by Him. *Why?* Because inspiration is manageable, but influence is not.

Comfortable Christians know when we have had too much Jesus. We need to be in control, to be inspired only, so that the world *still* loves us. We don't get lost in Him; we manage Him. We hear what He says, but we do what we want.

"Do not merely listen to the word, and so deceive yourselves. Do what it says." James 1:22

Isn't the purpose of hearing to prepare us for action? Just as a briefing identifies key objectives, when the 'hearing' is over, we're expected to fulfill the mission. But what if we like the briefing better than the mission? Picture a *007* film in which James Bond is more intrigued by receiving the assignment than completing its goals: *two hours of action packed briefings!*

James – the apostle, not Bond – is convinced that if we're going to 'hear,' then we should 'do' as well. But can you imagine if we did everything we heard? The lyrics of our favorite secular music artists suggest that we should sleep around, pop pills, and if necessary, commit drive-by shootings. We 'hear' for our enjoyment, *to be amused,* but not to act. *Hearing is entertainment;* we filter out what we're actually willing to do. Just as the media entertains us, we're also entertained by God. We're hearers, not doers.

EPIC FAIL

Right before every epic battle scene, the leader trots along the front lines. He yells out inspiring words to his men, preparing them to lay their lives down for their wives, their children, and their country! Few moments are more epic than a pre-battle speech. It prepares the men to give it their all in the face of death. They yell out a battle cry, and then *charge!!*

Imagine if the army didn't flinch as their leader rode into combat. Maybe they forgot the battle cry. Their leader returns in disarray. He repeats the scene, unites his men again, and with a cry rides into battle … alone. Again. Even if there were some willing, they were trapped behind the ranks of stagnant soldiers.

Paul tells us to be strong in the Lord, to put on the armor and fight against spiritual forces (Ephesians 6:11). We've heard the battle-cry, perhaps *every Sunday*. With spirits lifted, inspired by Jesus, for His kingdom, for our brothers and sisters, for the lost, we cry out! ... and then we don't flinch. *Epic fail.*

Jesus rides out solo. The willing warriors (who would overcome with love and not actual military force) are impeded by the stagnation and hypocrisy of Comfortable Christians. So He comes back and repeats the scene. Are we really His men, or are we here to be entertained?

DEDICATION TO INSPIRATION

Successful journeys begin with inspiration, as do failed ones. Inspiration itself has no outcome; it can only prompt. Without dedication, we'll need *repeated* prompting. For example, a car with a bad battery can run after getting a jump, but once the engine is turned off and it cools, it needs another jump.

Our walk with God may be inspired every time we go to church, hear a testimony, or listen to worship music. But these things can only prompt us. They don't provide us with the endurance to keep seeking. Perhaps our dedication is not to God, but to repeated inspiration.

We spend our whole lives trying to make it through the day, seeking the inspiration to keep going. But what if we tasked ourselves to jump others who are stalling, becoming the inspiration as opposed to seeking it? Let's draw closer to the Source and reflect His light to our world: our co-workers, friends and (God-forbid) enemies.

 Inspiring people is easy. Just tell 'em you'll pray for them, *even if you never will!*

THE SUPPLEMENT DIET

"Jesus answered, 'It is written: Man shall not live on bread alone, but on every word that comes from the mouth of God.'" Matthew 4:4

Inspiration is only a supplement. It can only compliment a proper diet, not replace it. Too often we depend on supplemental elements to nourish our spirit.

Inside of a nutrition store are many types of supplements and vitamins. What they don't have, however, is actual food. None of these supplements, either by themselves or in combination with other supplements, can replace a healthy diet. They're of no value if consumed improperly. We would only gain frustration if we took a diet pill with a burger, a protein shake without exercise, or a sleep aid without going to bed.

Likewise, being God inspired does no good *when it's in place* of actively seeking Him. It only results in frustrating highs and lows, being in constant need of more inspiration. Without nearing the Source, which takes discipline, we prevent ourselves from becoming the light of the world. The root of the issue is the disconnect: the separation between being the Lord's temple and having the Lord's mindset.

SEPARATION OF CHURCH AND STATE... OF MIND

"The mind governed by the flesh is hostile to God; it does not submit to God's law, nor can it do so." Romans 8:7

I was listening to a song by Macklemore that supports gay marriage. It's titled, *Same Love*, and the hook goes, "I can't change, even if I tried, even if I wanted to." The melody and lyrics are so convincing, it could melt the heart of the most homophobic bigot – *at least while it's playing*. It makes listeners sympathize for a historically alienated group in society that just can't change.

As Christians, can't we identify with it? After all, in our struggle with the flesh, many of us are falling for the same things over and over. The idea that, 'I can't change' sets in, or *I don't want to change.* This is who I am; this is my identity – this is what I love.

It begs the question, why should I change? Even if the desire to change came from within and not social pressure, it would take more than individual ability – it would take God's power. (Given that such a thing exists). Have we really submitted to Him – heart, mind, soul, and strength – *before* saying 'no' to the desires of the flesh? *I know I haven't.* It's easy to point out homosexuals because we can see what it is that they can't change – *if they wanted to.* But what is it that you can't change, if you wanted to?

The reason I bring up homosexuality again is not to hammer it, but to explore how something we can't change, *or don't want to change,* becomes our identity. What sin has become our identity? Are we fornicators, drunkards, or gossipers? If we are addicted to pornography, are we masturbators? Have we allowed sin to define us? All but a few sins are considered wrong in the eyes of the world. To them, sins are normal behaviors.

THE SPECIAL ONE

"Do not conform to the pattern of this world, but be transformed by the renewing of your mind. Then you will be able to test and approve what God's will is – his good, pleasing and perfect will." Romans 12:2

As children, we're told that we're all special. We're sold dreams about how we could become president and change the world. Instead, we grow up and the world changes us. *Silly dreams.* How can I change the world if I can't change myself? "...even if I tried, even if I wanted to." (Sorry, the song is stuck in my head.) We're all the same. There are seven billion people on the earth, and not even our desire to be special is special.

What makes some people great is their ability to transform. They stand out amongst us, and inspire us. They make us dream. "I wanna be like Mike" was a popular saying in the 90's, referring to the greatness of Michael Jordan. But many people don't realize that he was cut from his high school basketball team. He wasn't born great; *he became great.*

Greatness isn't a birthright. It's the realization of our potential, which is then directed to a transformation. It's a rebirth of oneself.

IN-IMMACULATE CONCEPTION

"Jesus replied, 'Very truly I tell you, no one can see the kingdom of God unless they are born again.'" John 3:3

Birth is an exciting time for parents. They have huge dreams for their kids. They want them to be better than they were; they want them to be great. Some envision their children as doctors, doctors, *or even* doctors. Others want them to be doctors. Occasionally, parents may want them to be their successors – depending on their own level of success – as there is little pressure to be a third generation janitor. "My father gave me this mop, now I give it to you. You will give it to your son."

The pressure often overwhelms children. They feel as though their parents seek to live vicariously through them. Many ultimately disappoint their families by falling short of those expectations.

I was the only child of two well-known, yet incredibly humble ministers within the Ethiopian community. Growing up, our home was open to all who needed prayer, counseling, and even exorcism. *Seriously, exorcism.* Our neighbors once frantically called because they heard demonic screaming from across the street. *Imagine trying to explain that.*

Oftentimes, people I didn't even know would tell me how their lives were changed because of my parents' ministry. They asked me if I was going to be a minister too – a chip off the old block. But that was the last thing on my mind. I just wanted to be a normal Christian: no preaching, no mission trips, and definitely no casting out demons!

Years after people stopped asking, I began to assess my life. I compared my flesh-led, self-gratifying life to my parents' Spirit-led, selfless lives. I wished that somehow, I could resemble them, in that respect. But even *if* I wanted to serve God, I couldn't envision myself becoming a fraction of the ministers that they were.

We often regard our pastors as holier, more spiritual, and overall greater Christians than we are, or will ever be. After all, they impact the lives of hundreds or thousands. But consider this: they're limited to their audiences. There are two billion Christians in the world; together, we have the ability to touch everyone! Our audience is the world.

"Very truly I tell you, whoever believes in me will do the works I have been doing, and they will do even greater things than these, because I am going to the Father." John 14:12

When we're born again, we have so much potential. Jesus called us to do greater things than He had done. He transforms our lives so that we can turn around and transform the lives of others. He reaches out to us so we can reach the world, not so we can be paralyzed with the notion that we can never be as great.

Jesus seeks to live vicariously through us, but instead, we conform to this world. We distance ourselves from the Family (Trinity) business. Instead of being fruitful, we remain as a single seed (John 12:24). As sons and daughters of God, we disappoint by falling short of our potential.

GREATNESS BEGINS IN THE MIND

Great people don't conform to great opposition. What separates people like Martin Luther King, Jr. from everyone is that they didn't respond the way a regular person would. For example, when he was hit with a brick while marching for civil rights, did he stop marching or try to find out who threw it, to retaliate? If that had happened to us, we may have.

When Jesus was being crucified, did He consider taking the life of those soldiers and religious leaders who mocked Him? We may have. After all, they were taunting Him to come down, if indeed He was the Son of God. Think of the humility it took not to. But if He had, *He'd be just like us.* It would be a normal reaction of someone who has conformed to this world.

One thief crucified alongside Jesus believed, and after the Lord died, a Roman soldier said, "Truly this man was the Son of God" (Mark 15:39). True greatness changes others.

We'll never be great in His kingdom if we impede the renewal of our minds. And many of us are comfortable with that –

comfortable not living up to the standard of Christ. It's a standard that requires the transformation of the mind.

LIVING IN HIGH DEFINITION

Life is so short, so unpredictable – not just for those who die young, but also for those who grow old drowning in everyday worries. We hope that after we die, we'll be remembered or defined by good things. Perhaps we want to be known as someone who was kind or loving – someone who always meant well. No one wants to be forgotten; we want something good to define our existence.

I can think of no greater honor than to be defined by Christ – to be spoken of as someone who not only believed in Jesus, but dedicated his life to His principles. When I die, I hope that people can say that I wasn't just a Christian, *but I was Christlike.*

I better not die now.

When people see the church, I pray that they can see Christ. I hope they can look past those who have misrepresented Him, including myself, and see that Jesus truly is the Way, the Truth, and the Life. But the reality is, when the world thinks of Christ, they think of us instead.

All I can do about this is examine myself – examine whether my faith is genuine, and encourage others to do the same. Is my life defined by Jesus? How can I transform my world, without first focusing on my own transformation?

PENDING METAMORPHOSIS

"Therefore, if anyone is in Christ, the new creation has come: The old has gone, the new is here!" 2 Corinthians 5:17

Christians are called to undergo a complete metamorphosis – to die to our old selves. When a caterpillar transforms into a butterfly, it not only changes its appearance, but also its actions.

But what if it left the cocoon without being fully transformed? What if it only had one wing, and the other half remained in a caterpillar state? It was supposed to go from being an ugly bug to a beautiful butterfly, but instead, it's uglier than it was in the first place! It becomes useless to both types of lives because it can't fly or crawl straight.

Many of us have partially transformed. Instead of becoming something to be admired, we have become some deformed Frankenstein version of Christ. We're useless to both types of lives, neither realizing our spiritual destiny or satisfying our fleshly desires.

"Those who live according to the flesh have their minds set on what the flesh desires; but those who live in accordance with the Spirit have their minds set on what the Spirit desires." Romans 8:5

As Christians, we know what's *off limits* for us, and we try to abstain from the things of the world. But abstinence must come as a byproduct of the renewal of our mind. Otherwise we're only attacking the symptoms of our flesh, and not our flesh itself.

For example, many medications only suppress our symptoms; they don't attack the virus we're suffering from. Painkillers don't attack the source of our pain; they only block the brain's signal that we're hurting. But we are hurting, we just can't tell because we're numb.

Comfortable Christianity is spiritual numbness.

MISSING YOUR VISION

"Then they gathered around him and asked him, 'Lord, are you at this time going to restore the kingdom of Israel?'" Acts 1:6

Up until the point that Jesus ascended into heaven, the disciples still didn't understand the vision of the Messiah. They were expecting Him to overthrow the Romans and restore an earthly kingdom. They were so close to Jesus, but they were still missing the vision. As He ascended into heaven, they were all looking up at the clouds. But the answer was no longer in the tangible God; it was to be in them, after they were transformed by the Spirit of Jesus.

Before Jesus ascended, He gave His disciples a command to be great, to transform the world with the Gospel. But He told them to first wait until they received power from the Holy Spirit. They would be transformed first, given the boldness, the strength, and ability to carry out the vision.

If you have a vision, it doesn't matter how far you are from it; you may ultimately find a way. But if you don't have a vision, it doesn't matter how close you are to it; you may never reach it. Many of us are missing Jesus's vision for our lives at point blank range. Our kingdom is not of this world. It's intangible, and we can only grasp it with a renewed mind – *a mind that is redirected and transformed by the Holy Spirit.*

ERASING THE PENTECOST

"They saw what seemed to be tongues of fire that separated and came to rest on each of them. All of them were filled with the Holy Spirit and began to speak in other tongues as the Spirit enabled them." Acts 2: 3-4

The Day of Pentecost occurred during a Jewish festival; many devout pilgrims had come from different nations to celebrate it. When the Holy Spirit came upon the disciples, they miraculously spoke in the native tongues of the pilgrims. *They were stunned.* How could these Galileans do this? But it was not them speaking; it was God speaking *through* them. That day, 3,000 people were born-again.

Imagine if the Holy Spirit never filled the disciples. What would have become of them after Christ's departure? How would they have witnessed to those pilgrims? *Perhaps they wouldn't have.* In fact, Peter may have denied Jesus a *fourth* time. Jesus told them He would send someone greater: the Holy Spirit.

But how can the Spirit of God be greater than a physical, tangible, miracle- working God? Well, up until the Day of Pentecost, Christ only *inspired* the disciples. They were *inspired* by His parables, teachings, and miracles. But they *still* didn't have the strength or the sense of urgency to be like Him.

For example, before Jesus was arrested in Gethsemane, He told them to stay up and pray. Instead, they slept. When the soldiers came, they scattered. They didn't have the ability to give up their lives, to be extensions of Jesus until the day of transformation – the day of Pentecost. No longer were they God-*inspired.* Now, they were God-*influenced.*

"When they arrived, they prayed for the new believers there that they might receive the Holy Spirit, because the Holy Spirit had not yet come on any of them; they had simply been baptized in the name of the Lord Jesus." Acts 8:15-16

The majority of Christians today have not seen miracles or Jesus. Picture us trying to be extensions of Jesus *without the empowerment of Jesus.* In essence, we're trying to do what the apostles could not. We're sleeping when we're called to be praying – never developing the ability to live for Christ.

The Holy Spirit reveals the spiritual warfare that goes on around us. We're often ignorant of these dark forces, *but they're not ignorant of us.* The devil can see when our light is dim, and he strives to keep us there. Rather than destroy us, his aim is to limit us, to keep us *comfortable,* so that we may have the form of godliness, but deny its power (2 Timothy 3:5). By failing to seek the Holy Spirit, we remain Christ-*inspired,* and never Christ-*influenced.*

"Not that I have already obtained all this, or have already arrived at my goal, but I press on to take hold of that for which Christ Jesus took hold of me. Brothers and sisters, I do not consider myself yet to have taken hold of it. But one thing I do: Forgetting what is behind and straining toward what is ahead, I press on toward the goal to win the prize for which God has called me heavenward in Christ Jesus." Philippians 3:12-14

POSTSCRIPT

As this self-reflective journey concludes, I ask myself, "Where do I go from here?" I also ask myself, "Where does the reader go from here?"

You see, when we began, I outlined the three objectives of this book. Its mission was to: 1) examine Christian hypocrisy from the eyes of a hypocrite, 2) explore genuine faith in contrast, and 3) encourage and compel transformation, beginning with my own. I trust that I have done a satisfactory job with the first two objectives, but what about the last?

Have I succeeded in the final objective – to compel my own change, to compel yours? Or do we both close this book enlightened, perhaps entertained, yet unmoved?

We often say, "God has a plan for your life," but the reality is, so does Satan. The devil has many angles – he may at times try to frustrate us, or keep us distracted. But the most vicious plan he imposes on us is comfort.

Comfort – it's a plan we rarely object. In fact, we strive to achieve it. We may even mistake comfort as a blessing. Clearly we are in God's plan if everything is going smoothly. *Right?*

The devil laughs. What greater tool is there to sterilize a Christian than to keep him/her content?

In *Screwtape Letters*, a senior-level devil advises a novice one in securing the soul of a newly Christian convert. When the novice demon seems to be losing grasp of the Christian, Screwtape writes, *"As long as he does not convert it into action, it does not matter how much he thinks about this new repentance. Let the little brute wallow in it. Let him, if he has any bent that way, write a book about it, that is often an excellent way of sterilizing the seeds which the Enemy [God] plants in a human soul. Let him do anything but act."*

My jaw dropped when I read this: I was in the middle of 'writing a book about it'. You see, repentance is just the beginning. If we never allow the Spirit's conviction to be converted into action, we've utterly failed.

I pray that neither you nor I become this devil's 'little brute.' I pray that this this examination of ourselves does not end in sterilization. If it does, we have played right into the hands of Screwtape – we've remained Comfortable Christians.

Special Thanks

I would like to thank the late Jon Randles. He was a great minister who came to my church camp year after year, challenging us. One year, it finally clicked, and not only did I make a dramatic change in my life, but I immediately began writing this book. I'll never forget the way he lit up when I told him about it. Unfortunately, he passed away before the book was complete.

I'd like to thank my wife Netsanet Seifu for her support throughout the entirety of this project, and most of all, for believing in me. This process would have been impossible without her faith, love, and encouragement.

I'd like to thank my parents, Seifu Kebede and Tsigie Tekleab, who have invested so much into me. After all these years, I have something to show for it. I know they wanted me to become a pastor like them, but God had another plan... and it took some time for that plan to come to pass because of my hard-headedness.

I'd like to thank Justin Dickson, who upon learning that I had begun writing this book, encouraged me to complete it by saying I'd be committing a sin if I didn't. He always pushed me and believed that my humor could be used to do something big that would touch people's lives.

I'd like to thank Nati Tessema for helping me shape and edit the book. His criticism, while at times frustrating, always pushed me to write better. He never let anything slide—a true friend.

I'd like to thank Ida Legesse for her help, especially with editing the first draft—*it was really a rough copy*. I'll never forget those grueling weeks she spent with me. Her time, effort, and encouragement throughout the process was priceless.

I'd like to thank Lina Woldemariam not only her help revising the book and the study guide, but also for her encouraging attitude that helped me get through difficult times.

I'd like to thank my illustrator, Dag Haile, for his creativity, skill, and help in the production of this book.

I'd like to thank my editor, Lindsay Morris. I truly believe that God arranged my meeting with her. It was so invaluable that I not only had a capable editor, but one who cared just as much about the book as I did—or at least made me believe that was the case! She made the most daunting part of this process seem like a breeze.

I'd like to thank Nathan Araya. Since the beginning, he has supported and challenged me. And in the end, he spent a lot of time working with me and helping me get the message out. His input was invaluable.

I'd like to thank Isayas Theodros. I can't really express how essential he has been to this book and to me personally. He edited the book not just once, but a year later, twice. He went above and beyond the call of close friend, and he believed in me even when I didn't.

I'd like to thank my church, Ethiopian Christian Fellowship and all the wonderful people there who truly cared and were excited for this.

Finally, I'd like to thank God for making me a vessel—despite my ill-qualification. All things done for Him are through Him, and I'm blessed to be a part of the plan.